# MANNHEIM STEAMROLLER
*Christmas*

ARRANGED BY: CHIP DAVIS

Solo Piano Reduction and Editing by Jackson Berkey,
featured Keyboardist with Mannheim Steamroller.

*Full score and parts available for keyboards and orchestra
for "Bring A Torch, Jeanette, Isabella" and "Renaissance
Christmas Sweet."*

*Contact American Gramaphone Records for
details 402-457-4341*

# MANNHEIM STEAMROLLER
*Christmas*

## RENAISSANCE CHRISTMAS SWEET

# Deck the Halls

Arranged by Chip Davis

20

24

28

32

36

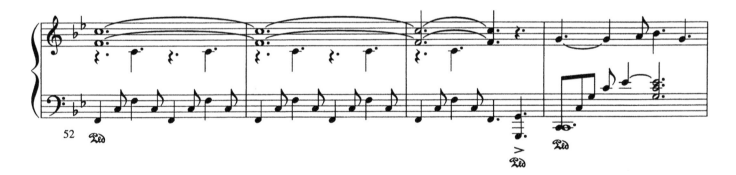

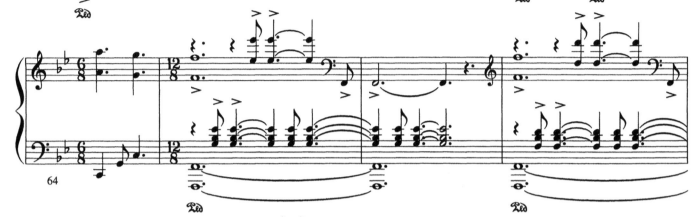

100

104

108

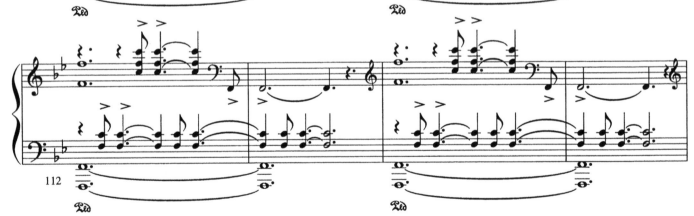

112

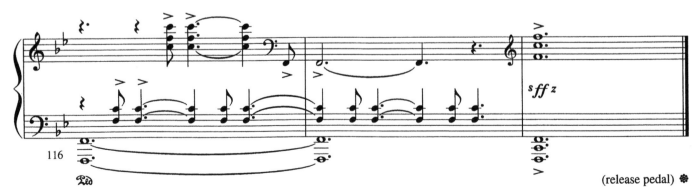

116

(release pedal) ❀

# We Three Kings

Arranged by Chip Davis

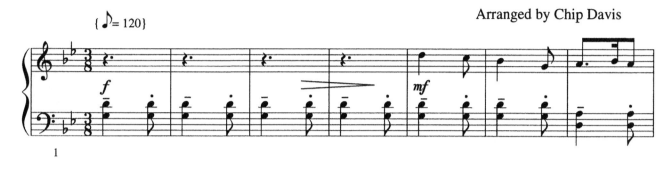

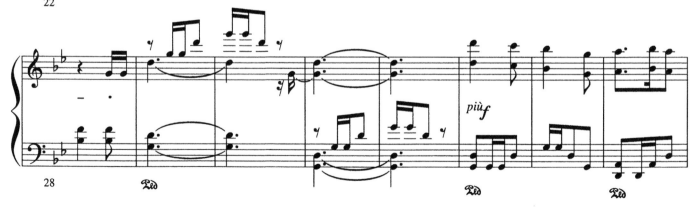

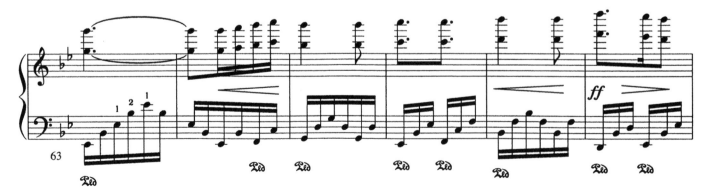

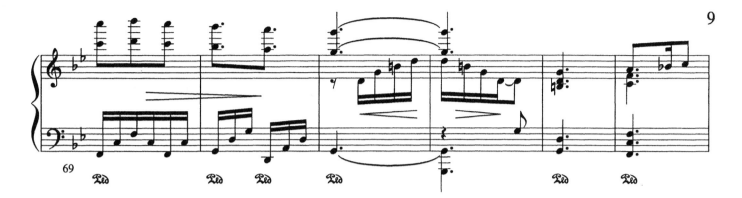

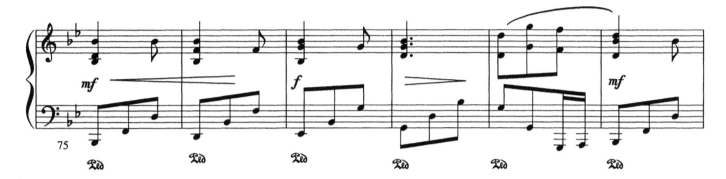

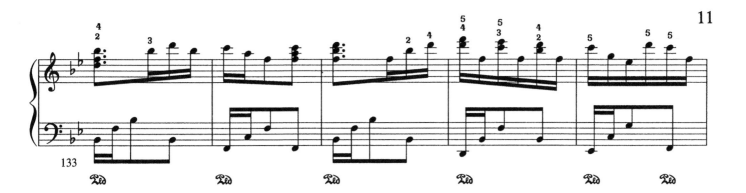

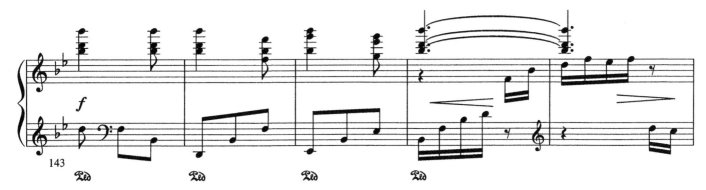

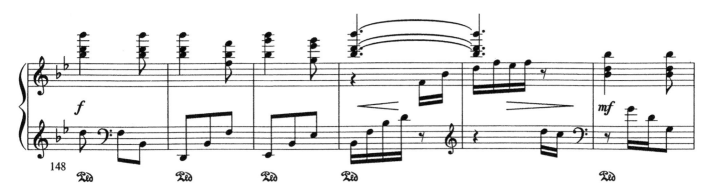

# Bring a Torch, Jeannette, Isabella

Arranged by Chip Davis

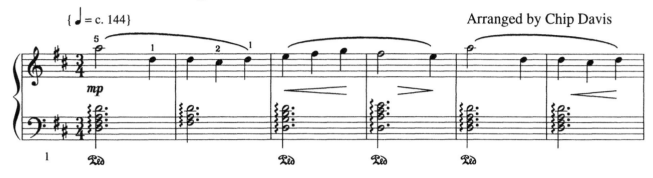

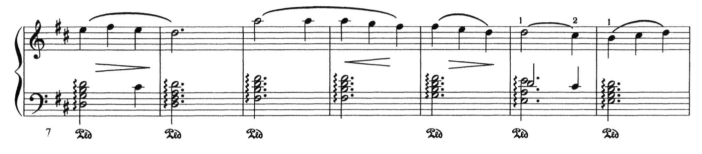

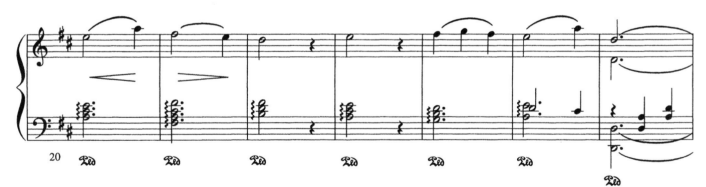

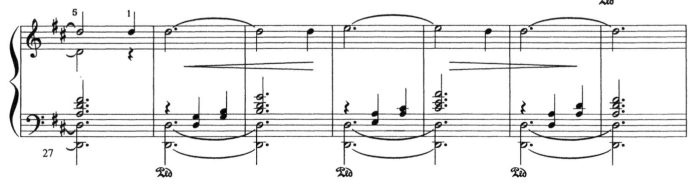

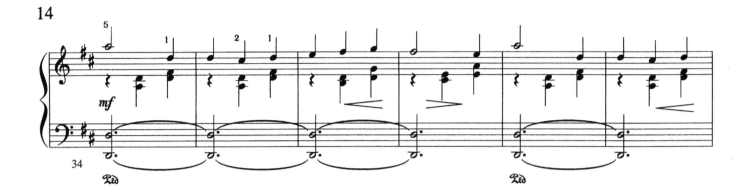

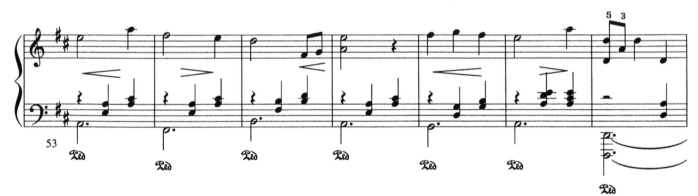

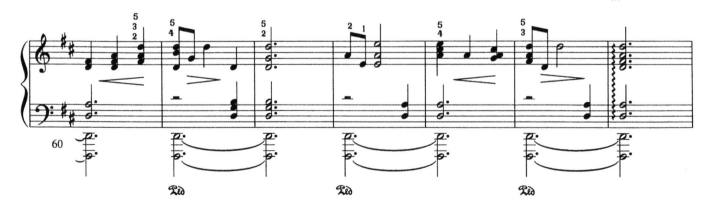

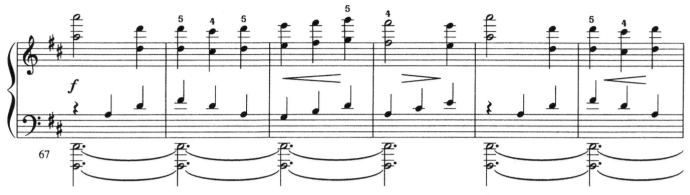

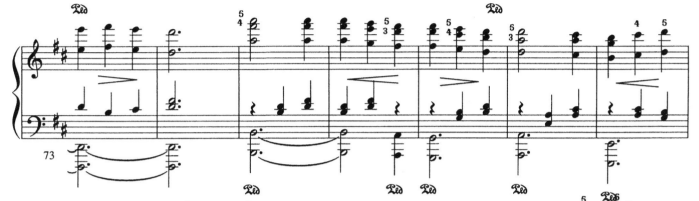

# Coventry Carol

Arranged by Chip Davis

harmonic changes throughout

(like an echo)

35

42

50

55

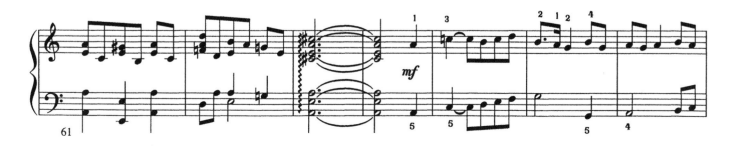

61

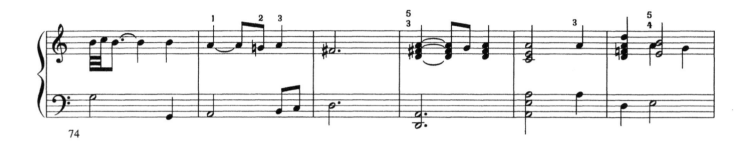

# Good King Wenceslas

( ♩ = c. 88}

Arranged by Chip Davis

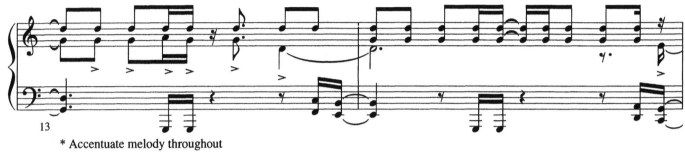

\* Accentuate melody throughout

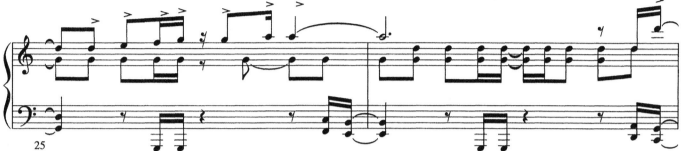

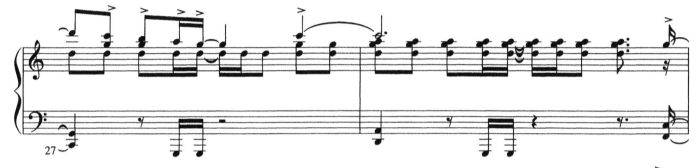

24

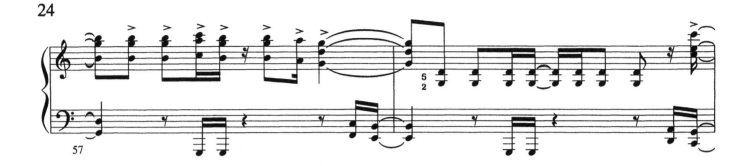

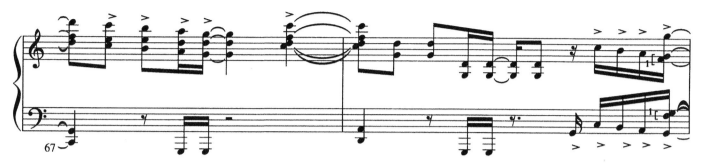

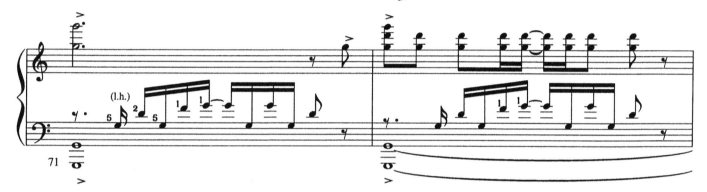

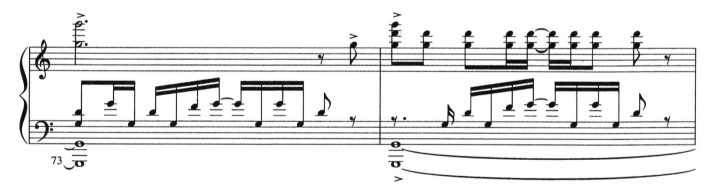

# Wassail, Wassail

Arranged by Chip Davis

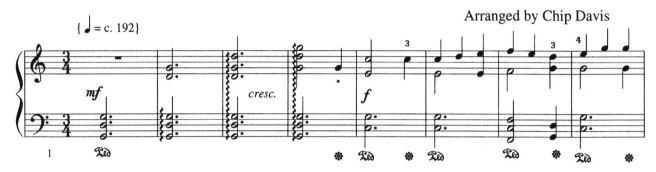

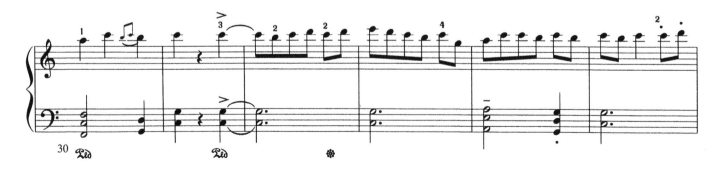

71

76

82

88

93

99

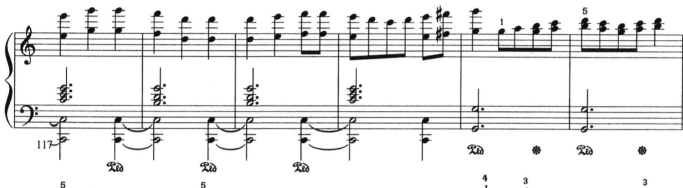

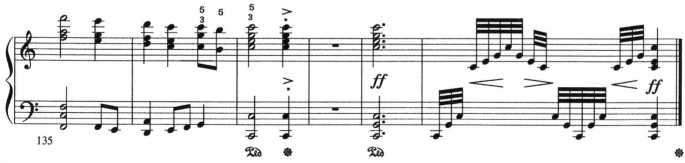

# Carol of the Birds

Arranged by Chip Davis

23

27

31

35

39

# I Saw Three Ships

Arranged by Chip Davis

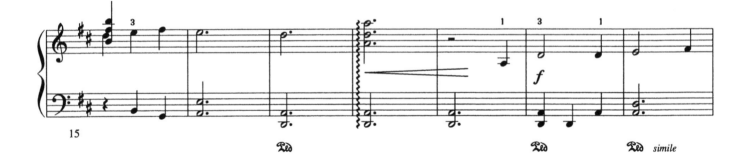

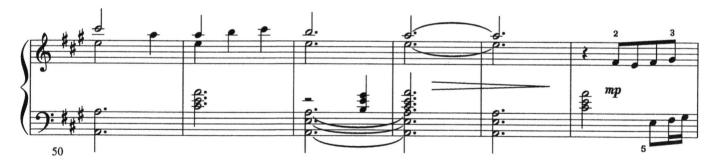

34

61

66

71

78

85

# God Rest Ye Merry, Gentlemen

*(Renaissance)*

Arranged by Chip Davis

37

43

49

55

62

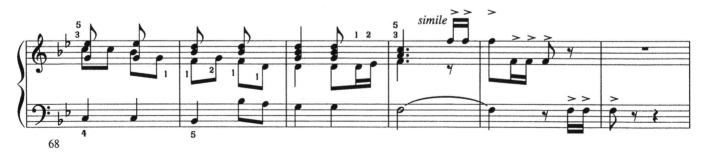

68

74

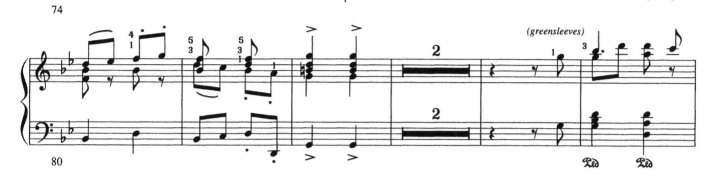

80

(greensleeves)

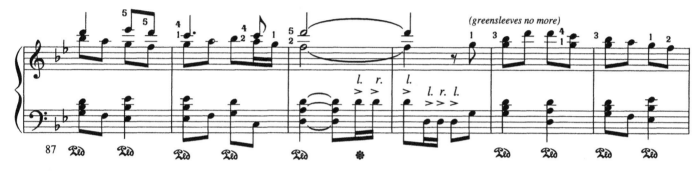

87

(greensleeves no more)

93

simile

99

simile

105

ff

# God Rest Ye Merry, Gentlemen

### (Rock 'n' Roll)

Arranged by Chip Davis

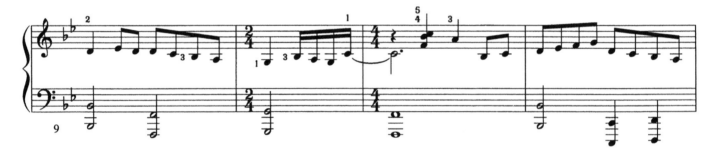

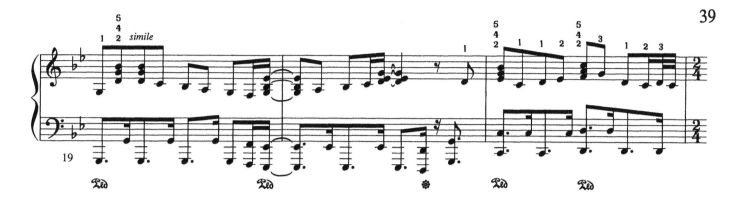

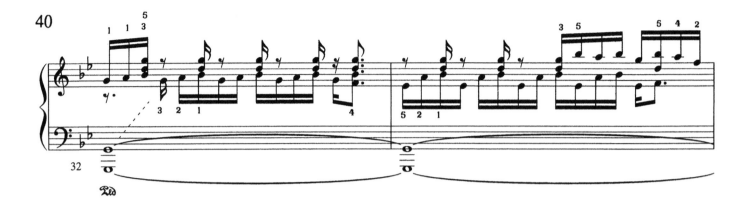

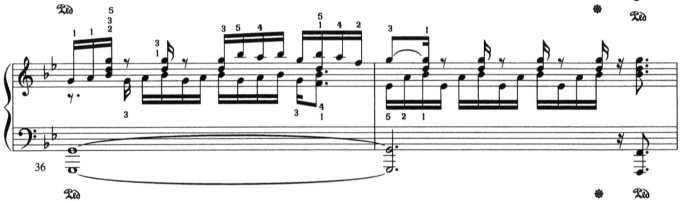

*less separated*

℗ℰ𝒹 melodic and harmonic motion

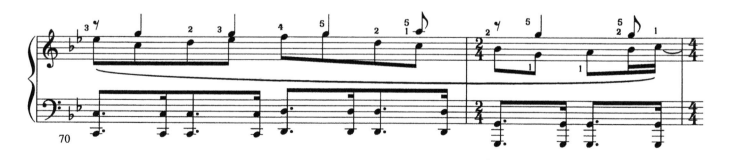

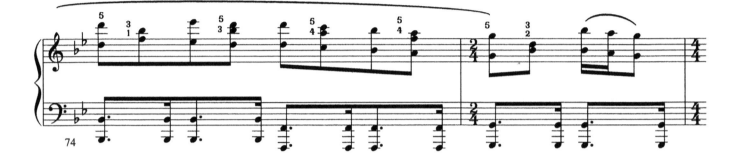

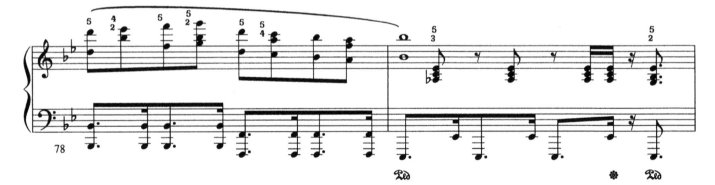

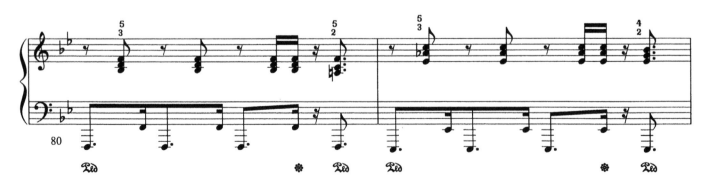

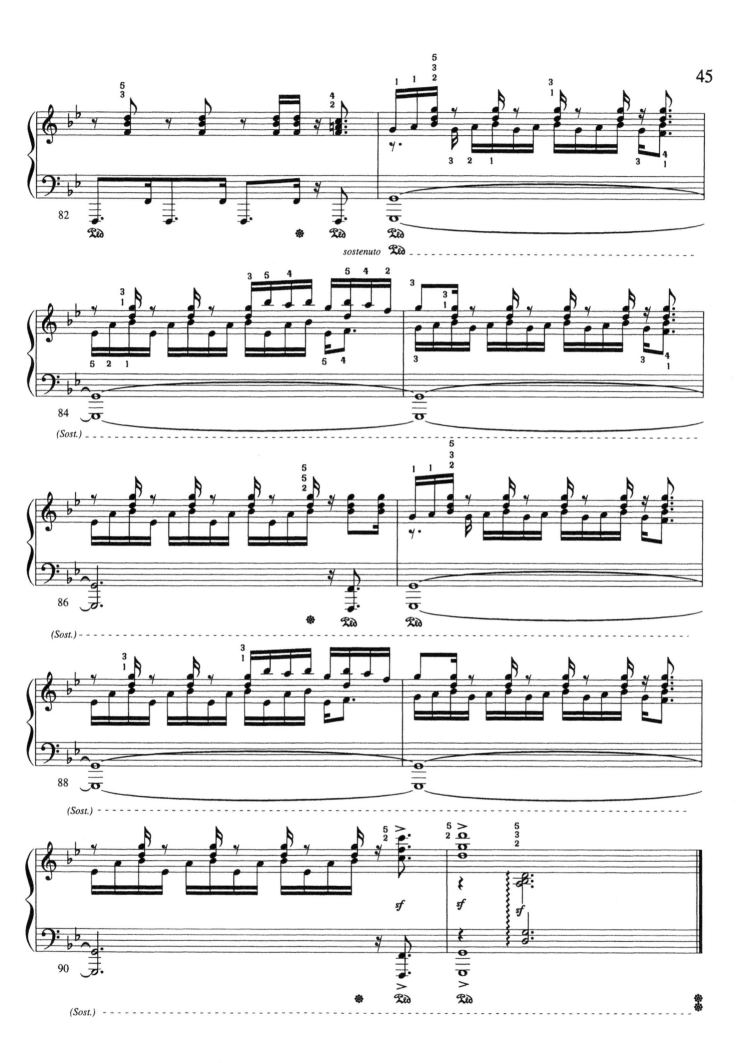

# Silent Night

Arranged by Chip Davis

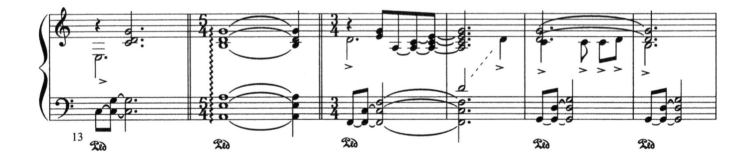

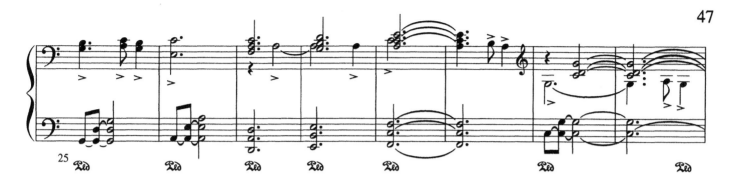

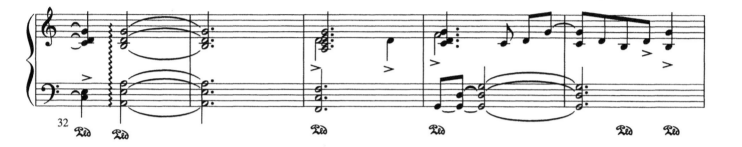

**a tempo espressivo**

52

*finger simile*

57

*finger simile*

62

67

72

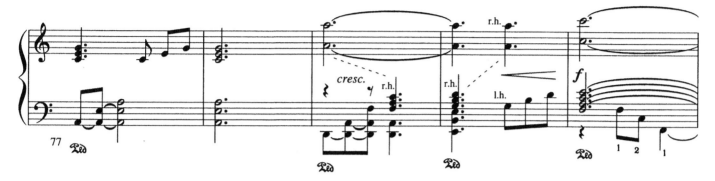

**Tempo di "Embers"**

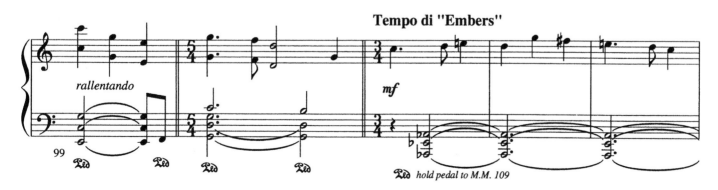

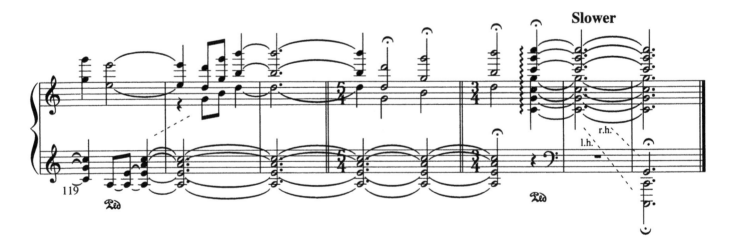

## DECK THE HALLS
### Welsh Ayre

An old Welsh carol, Deck the Halls, was from the ancient festival of celebrating the Yule. The celebration took place around the same time as Christmas and this song became popularly associated with Christmas. It was probably a dance song used while decorating the interior, eating plum pudding and drinking from the Wassail Bowl.

## WE THREE KINGS
### John Hopkins 1857

The three kings were Melchior, Caspar and Balthazar, and were guided by the star of Bethlehem to the Christ Child, as the legend goes. This is neither an ancient, nor a carol from the Orient as the name implies, but rather, an American carol written by John Hopkins Jr. in 1857, retelling the legend as it's known.

## BRING A TORCH, JEANNETTE, ISABELLA
### 17th Century French

This is a beautiful old 17th century French carol. I thought that the innocence of the alto recorder and the beauty of a full string section best portrayed the simplicity, and get the depth of this old tune.

## THE COVENTRY CAROL
### 16th Century English

This carol was originally from the mid 1400's, however, the melody as it is in this version, is derived from a later version in 1591.

I chose to set the harmonic structure and instrumental color as closely to the period as I could. In this case, the guitar probably would have been a lute, and the harpsichord, of course, is itself.

## GOOD KING WENCESLAS
### Traditional English Carol

The good king was Wenceslas of Bohemia, who ruled in the 10th century. The melody, which was used to sing about the good king, was a Swedish melody.

I have no idea why I chose to do such a silly rhythmic treatment of this, but we sure had fun recording it.

## WASSAIL, WASSAIL
### Ancient English Carol

This is an ancient English carol and I chose to set this in the renaissance style to further give the period feel from which it comes. I always found it to be a very "up" song and thought renaissance dance form would be the best. As in many of those arrangements, I've tried to extend them by adding new sections but making them sound as if these were the original versions.

## CAROL OF THE BIRDS
### Bas-Quercy

As the origin of many carols are from ancient pagan times, this one is an ancient French melody with the text being about a flock of birds that flew to the manger to bring gifts. It seemed to fit best in the renaissance style with recorders representing the birds.

## I SAW THREE SHIPS
### 15th Century Legend

There are some who say that the number of 3 ships is related to the three wise men. Being an English carol and England being at sea, it is about gifts being brought by sea reminiscent of the gifts brought by the three wise men. It is of 15th century origin which of course made it a natural for this renaissance "sweet."

## GOD REST YOU, MERRY
## GENTLEMEN
### English Carol

This Yuletide phrase is often printed – and sung – with this punctuation and the pause it implies. But that's not the way the charming old carol has it. Properly, It's "God rest you merry, gentlemen." The phrase "rest you merry," which is older than Shakespeare, who used it in **Romeo and Juliet**, dates to the beginning of the 15th century. Incidentally, the Old English word for "merry" did not mean gay and lively, but merely pleasant or agreeable. By the 14th century, however, it had acquired its present meaning.

This was arranged as a roundal. Roundals were called that  because they were songs presented at dinner parties on the back of the plates (round).

As each guest turned over their plate, they would sing their part and add to the Round. This piece is only about :30 seconds in length and was recorded vertically, each part at a time and then made to length by mixing out each part and adding it to create the various verses. Instead of a lot of guests at dinner around the table, it was just us.

## GOD REST YE MERRY,
## GENTLEMEN
### English Carol

I thought that since my whole writing game has been juxtaposition of old and new, it would be fun to do the same tune twice...old and...new.

DRUMSET INSTRUCTION

# INDEPENDENCE ON THE DRUMSET

## Coordination Studies for Drummers in All Styles

BY RICKY SEBASTIAN

Front cover photo by Dan Maske
Back cover photo by Davis Sokol

ISBN 0-634-09151-4

HAL•LEONARD®
CORPORATION
7777 W. BLUEMOUND RD. P.O. BOX 13819 MILWAUKEE, WI 53213

In Australia Contact:
**Hal Leonard Australia Pty. Ltd.**
22 Taunton Drive  P.O. Box 5130
Cheltenham East, 3192  Victoria, Australia
Email:  ausadmin@halleonard.com

Visit Hal Leonard Online at
**www.halleonard.com**

# ABOUT THE AUTHOR

Ricky Sebastian was born in Opelousas, Louisiana. He attended the University of Southwestern Louisiana on a full scholarship and later attended Berklee College of Music in Boston. He returned to New Orleans in 1976 and started working professionally. In 1983, he moved to New York City where he built a career as an in-demand recording and touring artist that spanned 16 years. Ricky moved back to New Orleans in 1999 and was an instructor at the University of New Orleans under the direction of Ellis Marsalis for 6 years. He returned to New York in 2004 and is currently on the teaching staff at Drummers Collective and the New School. He has recently released his first CD as a leader entitled "The Spirit Within" on STR Digital Records featuring the likes of Donald Harrison Jr., Bill Summers, Steve Masakowski, Randy Brecker, and Peter Martin.

Ricky can be reached by email at *ricseb@cox.net*

Website: *www.strdigital.com*

## Endorsements

Zildjian Cymbals
Pearl Drums
Pro-Mark Drumsticks
LP Percussion
Audix Microphones
Remo Products

# ACKNOWLEDGMENTS

There have been many people in my life that I would like to acknowledge for their help and guidance on my path through my playing and teaching career: My parents, my Grandmother Pearl, Carl DeLeo, Carl Schexnayder, Bill Poche, Hollis Fulton, James Black, John Vidacovich, Dr. John, Billy Hart, Jaco Pastorius, Paul Siegal, Rob Wallis, Earl and Willie Turbinton, George Porter Jr., Tony Notifonso, Gary Chaffe, Alan Dawson, John Scofield, Herbie Mann, Tania Maria, Dianne Reeves, Ellis Marsalis, Tony Williams, Elvin Jones, Max Roach, Steve Gadd, Philly Joe Jones, Harry Belafonte, Sergio Brandao, Mike and Randy Brecker, Alex Foster, Al Foster, Delmar Brown, Kenwood Dennard, Lenny White, Billy Cobham, Bill Summers, Edison "Café" DeSilva, Cyro Baptista, Paul Socolow, and Romero Lubambo.

It is my sincere hope that you will find many things to work on in this book to last you for a long time. I cannot stress enough, the importance of listening to the great drummers that have come before you, no matter what style of music you choose to play. And remember; keep practicing!

*In memory of Carl DeLeo and Carl Schexnayder.*

# CONTENTS

# INTRODUCTION

I grew up in a very musical home. My parents were excellent dancers and loved soul and cajun/zydeco music, so there was always something playing on the stereo. One day my dad bought a Zenith turntable and it came with several albums, one being a compilation jazz record. I was too young at the time to understand the music on this album, so I didn't listen to it. When I was around five years old, the Beatles hit America like a hurricane. Oddly enough, I wanted to be Paul McCartney, but started making a drumset out of boxes and some of my mother's old pots and pans. My grandmother saw this and, as a Christmas gift, gave me a toy set of drums (the kind that came in one big box). I'll never forget that day. Unfortunately, the heads were made of paper so I literally destroyed the set in one week, but that little set instilled in me a love and passion for drumming that still exists to this day.

When I was thirteen years old, my mother took me to a record store and I bought two albums, one by the group Yes and one by Jimi Hendrix. I listened to those records so many times that I wore them out. I started taking snare drum lessons at age eight in a small Catholic school which was so poor that we had to play on fold out metal chairs because they couldn't afford to buy marching drums. On the first day there were fifteen kids. When they realized that they had to learn to read music, the second day saw only five kids in the class. The band director, Carl DeLeo, saw that I had natural talent for the drums and spent extra time after class instructing me. His passion for teaching only fueled my interest in drumming. When I turned eleven, my dad bought my first snare drum, a Ludwig aluminum snare, and I was elated. When I turned thirteen, he took me to a pawn shop in New Orleans and bought a drumset, one with a red sparkle finish, no hi-hat, and no brand name. It only had a bass drum, one tom, one floor tom, and one cymbal. I was in heaven! Even at that age, though I had become a very proficient reader and knew all of the American rudiments, I was shocked the first time I sat down to play the drumset. I thought it would be easy, but I had never used my feet to play, only my hands in marching band. This challenge just made my desire to play grow even more. Since we lived in a small town in Louisiana, there were no drumset teachers available, so I started learning to play by ear, playing along with my favorite records from bands/artists like Jimi Hendrix, Yes, Led Zeppelin, Black Sabbath, and Grand Funk Railroad. I was a total rocker at this point. But by the time I got to high school, I had moved on to listening to progressive rock. Groups like Yes; King Crimson; and Emerson, Lake, and Palmer; plus all of the R&B and soul records that my parents had.

During this time I was also playing in the high school symphony orchestra. I played all of the instruments. Timpani was my favorite, but I also played mallets and all of the other classical percussion instruments. We had one of the top high school bands in the state and won many All-Parish and All-State awards.

At seventeen, I was awarded a full scholarship to the University of Southwest Louisiana and attended that school for one year. It was frustrating because there was no drumset teacher there either. The band director gave me my own room to set up my drums to practice and kept giving me books, but I wanted an instructor who could play drumset. So I ended up going to Berklee College of Music in Boston when I was nineteen. That experience changed my life. I studied with three different drumset teachers, and they were all teaching some of Alan Dawson's concepts. In just one semester, I improved so much that I was able to move to New Orleans and start working professionally with many great local musicians. At this point, I was heavily into fusion: Chick Corea's *Return to Forever*, Mahavishnu Orchestra, Weather Report, etc. I was also checking out bebop, but not understanding it yet. Then one day I bought Stanley Clarke's first solo album with Tony Williams on drums. Tony's playing in that context just blew my mind—I was able to relate to it and understand what he was doing. Then I started to backtrack and got heavily into bebop, listening to John Coltrane, Miles Davis, Clifford Brown/Max Roach, and pretty soon, I was buying all of the bebop records I could get my hands on. I was twenty at that time and started getting jazz gigs in New Orleans with the likes of Earl Turbinton, Ellis Marsalis, Steve Masakowski, Emily Remler, and other local jazz heroes.

I stayed in New Orleans for six years playing with just about every top musician in town, while getting interested in all types of music. New Orleans is a wonderful city to be in if you are learning to play the drums. It has a legacy of being a drum and trumpet town! I was playing jazz, funk, New Orleans traditional music, Second Line, Avant-Garde, and began my fascination with Latin music at this time.

After six years, I knew it was time to move on. Most of my musical idols lived in New York City. So, at the age of twenty five, I packed my bags and drums, and moved there. It was the greatest adventure of my life, and I ended up staying there for sixteen years playing with all of my idols, except Miles Davis. Fortunately for me, I had played with Dr. John a few times in New Orleans. He was living in New York, so I called him and he gave me my first big time gig and helped me get started. Billy Hart also let me sit in one night at a club called 55 Grand which was right down the street from where I was living. I would go there every night and meet musicians that were either performing or hanging out. When Billy let me sit in, that started the ball rolling and my name started to get around town via word of mouth.

At about this time, Paul Siegal, one of the owners of the world renowned school Drummer's Collective, approached me after a gig with Dr. John and asked if I would be interested in teaching there. It was the beginning of a thirteen year teaching career. Through teaching, I continued to learn and quickly realized that independence on the drumset was a crucial step in learning to play any style of music. As a result, I started to develop a system to teach independence to my students. Everything that I taught was written out by hand—I used no books. That experience was to become the nucleus for this book, and I am grateful and blessed to have had that experience and the chance to record and tour with some of the greatest musicians in the world.

In June of 2003, while teaching at the University of New Orleans, I decided that it was time to organize all of the hand-written material that I had been teaching into a book. This is the result. I sincerely hope you get as much out of this book as I did from the teachers I had. An instructor can only show you the way, but you must do the work. Practicing on a daily basis and listening to the great drummers is essential to success in this very competitive field.

Enjoy!

*Ricky Sebastian*

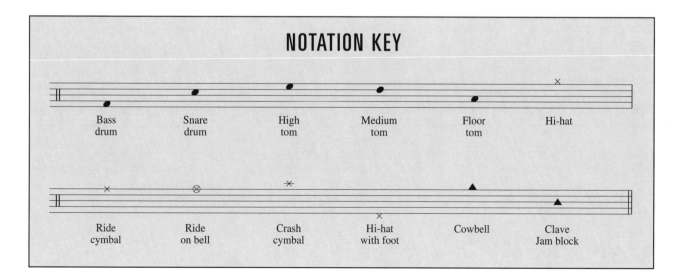

# 1 JAZZ/SWING APPLICATIONS

After a career as a professional drummer and instructor that has spanned twenty-five years, it has become clear to me that one of the most difficult aspects the drumset has to do with independence. What I mean by independence is this: the ability to play an ostinato (a one or two measure rhythm that repeats indefinitely) with one or two limbs, while playing something different with the other limbs over the ostinato. No matter the style, whether it be rock or jazz, Afro-Cuban or Brazilian, funk or calypso, you will encounter independence issues which require practice to be able to execute all of the parts together. The following exercises will give you a system of practice with which to gain mastery of independence on the drumset. In this book, you will find many different ostinatos which will be organized by letters starting with letter A. You will also find 240 different rhythmic (independence) patterns, each consisting of one measure, organized by numbers. There are endless ways of applying these rhythms as we will explore shortly. The goal, no matter what application you are practicing, is to play each independence pattern four times over a particular ostinato, then move to the next pattern without stopping until you reach the end and have played all 240 patterns. All of the independence patterns are located at the back of the book, beginning on page 58. You may wish to photocopy these pages (58-64) and mount them on the wall or another, stand for easier use.

We will start with jazz and a basic swing rhythm as the ostinato.

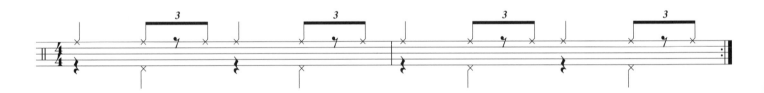

A note about interpreting jazz eighth notes. The swing ostinato has a triplet feel as opposed to a straight eighth note feel. So you must interpret the eighth notes in the independence patterns accordingly. Number one, below, shows how the music would be notated. Number two indicates how it is actually played.

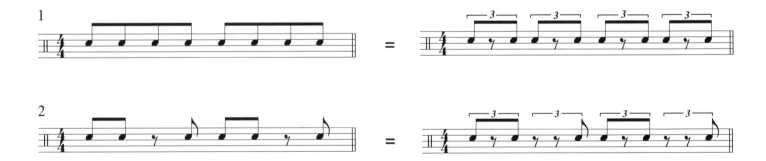

## One-Bar Phrases

**A** In this first application, start out by playing the independence patterns on the snare drum, along with the swing ostinato. The example below shows what this would look like using pattern 8 (see page 58 for all independence patterns).

**Track 1 plays patterns 1—45 on the bass drum with swing ostinato. Each pattern is played four times.**

TRACK 1

Pattern 8

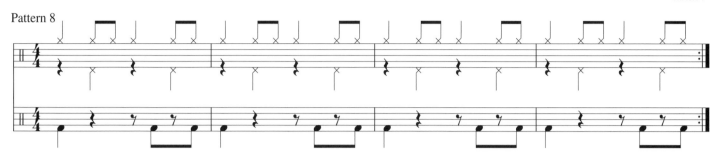

Play all 240 patterns with the above ostinato, each one four times, until you reach the end. If you encounter a pattern that is giving you problems, stop and practice that particular pattern until you have mastered it, then move on to the next one.

**B** Play all of the patterns on the bass drum with the swing ostinato.

**Track 2 plays patterns 1—21 on the bass drum with swing ostinato. Each pattern is played four times.**

TRACK 2

Pattern 9

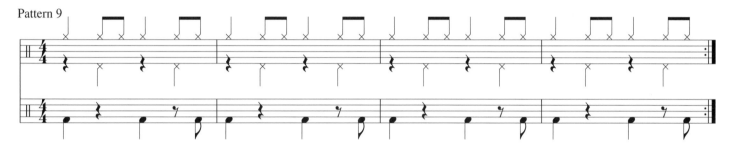

**C** Play the swing ostinato on the ride cymbal and the independence patterns on the hi-hat with your foot.

**Track 3 plays patterns 22-45 with hi-hat (foot), along with swing ride.**

TRACK 3

Pattern 10

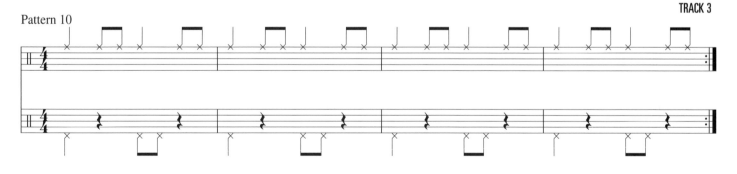

By now, you should be at a point where you understand the system presented to you in this book. We will continue with jazz applications for now. Later in the book, we will move on to other applications as well as different styles of drumming.

In the next section, we will start to use two voices on the drums instead of one voice. In jazz, phrases are played on the bass drum, snare drum, and hi-hat primarily, but many drummers also use toms, cymbals, etc., for orchestrating these improvisational phrases. After all, the purpose of these exercises is to achieve the ability to play time (in this case, swing) while playing improvisational ideas with the left hand, right foot, and left foot (snare drum, bass drum, hi-hat). We will continue to explore these possibilities in the next few pages.

D    Play the quarter notes on the bass drum and the eighth notes on the snare drum with the swing ostinato.

**Track 4 patterns 46–49 with swing osinato.**

Pattern 8

E    Now, reverse the above process. Play the quarter notes on the snare drum and the eighth notes on the bass drum with the swing ostinato.

Pattern 8

F    Let's get the hi-hat involved. Play the quarter notes on the hi-hat with your foot and the eighth notes on the snare drum with the swing ostinato (ride cymbal only).

Pattern 7

G    Next, reverse application F and play the quarter notes on the snare drum and the eighth notes on the hi-hat with your foot, along with the swing ostinato (ride cymbal only).

Pattern 28

H    In this application, play the quarter notes on the hi-hat with your foot and the eighth notes on the bass drum, with the ride cymbal playing the swing ostinato. After that, switch—quarter notes on the bass drum and eighth notes on the hi-hat.

By now, you should have a good understanding of how this practice system works. We will continue with applications, and only show a transcription of the pattern when necessary.

Play the independence patterns on the bass drum. Fill in the rests (or the space after each bass drum attack) with triplets on the snare drum (with the left hand), while keeping the swing ostinato on the cymbal and hi-hat. This is an excellent exercise to develop left-hand technique.

Pattern 8

Reverse the instruments and play the patterns on the snare drum, filling in the rests with triplets on the bass drum, along with the swing ostinato.

Pattern 8

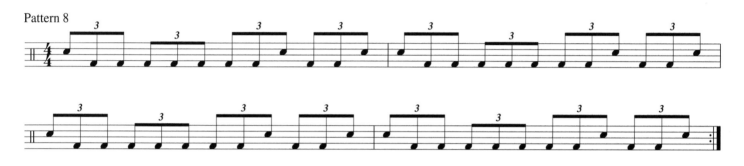

To take it even further, play the quarter notes on the hi-hat, the eighth notes on the bass drum, fill in the rests with triplets on the snare drum with your left hand, and play the swing ostinato on the ride cymbal only.

Pattern 29

While playing quarter note triplets on the snare drum, execute the independence patterns on the bass drum along with the swing ostinato on cymbal and hi-hat.

Pattern 14 (bottom staff)

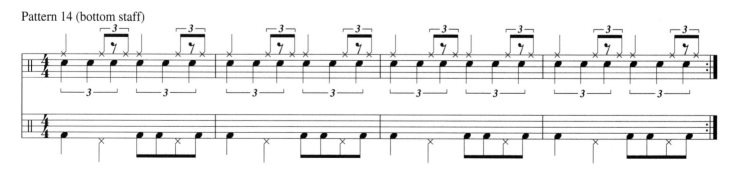

Remember to swing the eighth notes on the bass drum and ride cymbal.

**M**  Reverse the instruments in application L. Play quarter note triplets on the bass drum along with the swing ostinato and play the independence patterns on the snare drum.

**N**  Play the reverse side of the quarter note triplet on the snare drum along with the swing ostinato and play the independence patterns on the bass drum. Note: the eighth notes in the lower staff represent where the quarter-note triplets were played in application L. In example N, we are now playing in between those.

Pattern 3

**O**  Using the exercise from application N, play the reverse side of the quarter note triplet on the bass drum along with the swing ostinato and play the independence patterns on the snare drum. You can also play quarter note triplets on the hi-hat with your foot along with the swing ostinato on the ride cymbal only. Then, on the independence patterns, play the quarter notes on the bass drum and the eighth notes on the snare drum, and vice versa.

## Two-Bar Phrases

In jazz, rhythmic phrasing is paramount to the style. Though many phrases can be one measure in length, the majority of jazz phrasing uses at least two measures or more. Often, a rhythmic phrase will end "over the bar line," or, to put it another way, the phrase will start on beat one of the first measure and end on the "and" of beat three in the second measure. The possibilities are infinite. This is one of the beautiful concepts of improvisation and playing jazz, in general. Using the independence patterns with the swing ostinato, the following is a system of practice that will help you to develop this concept. We will be using two voices in this exercise, the snare drum and the bass drum. Read the patterns, playing the quarter notes on the bass drum and the eighth notes on the snare drum, then vice-versa. The idea is to combine two patterns to make a two measure rhythmic phrase. This is how the system works. Using the swing ostinato, combine patterns 1 and 2, and play this two measure phrase two times. Then combine pattern 1 with pattern 3 and play this phrase two times. Next, combine pattern 1 with 4, then 1 with 5. Continue in this fashion until you have combined pattern 1 with all 240 patterns. Then you can take pattern 2 and use it as the first measure, combining it with patterns 1, 2, 3, etc., until you've reached pattern 240. Use each successive pattern as the first measure and combine it with all the other patterns. You can reverse the process and use pattern 240 as the first measure combining it with 239, then 238, and move backwards until you've combined 240 with 1. The possibilities are infinite—use your imagination and combine patterns in any way that you like, to make up 2 measure phrases. Following are some examples:

TRACK 5    TRACK 6

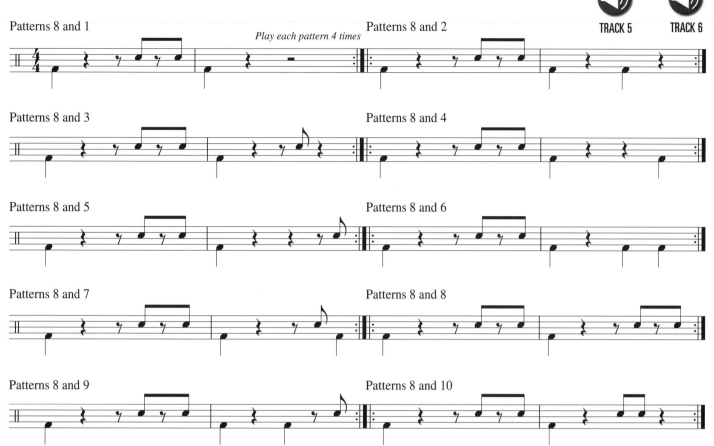

## Over-the-Bar Phrases

Many phrases that drummers play are based off of the dotted quarter note. This enables one to play a rhythmic phrase over the bar line, into the next measure. In the exercises below, play the patterns first on the snare drum, then play them on the bass drum, both times with the swing ostinato. The next step is to play the quarter notes on the bass drum and the eighth notes on the snare drum, then vice-versa.

**Track 7 plays patterns 1–7.**

TRACK 7

Practice all of these "over-the-bar line" exercises at medium, medium fast, and fast tempos to have control playing these types of phrases at any speed. You can also change your ride cymbal pattern to move with the dotted quarter note phrases accordingly. For example, the above patterns repeat themselves every three beats. Thus, you can play a pattern on the ride that also repeats itself every three beats as in the first example below. This causes the pattern to start on different beats in each measure since the meter indicates four beats per measure.

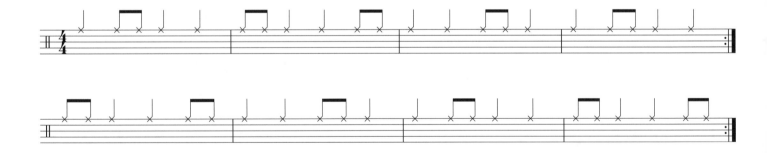

# 2 STRAIGHT EIGHTH NOTES (NON-SWING) APPLICATIONS

In this chapter, the ostinatos that we will be dealing with all have a straight eighth-note feel to them (played as written). So, you must interpret the independence patterns accordingly. As in chapter 1, ostinatos will be organized by letters and patterns organized by numbers.

## Bass Drum Development

A Play eighth notes on the bass drum while playing the hi-hat on beats 1, 2, 3, and 4 with your foot. Play the independence patterns as accents on the bass drum. This is an extraordinary exercise to develop control over the bass drum pedal.

**Track 8 plays patterns 1–21.**

TRACK 8

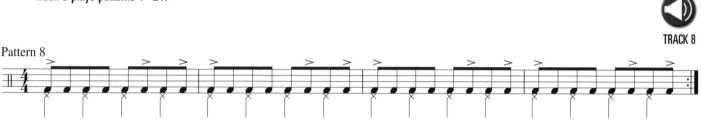

B Play application A, but play the hi-hat with your foot on beats 1 & 3 only. Then try application A again, with the hi-hat playing on beats 2 & 4.

C This is the same as application B, but with a shuffle (triplet) feel. It is desirable to have control of the bass drum in both feels. The shuffle feel is commonly used in hip hop and rap, as well as certain types of funk and R&B.

## Latin Patterns with Cowbell

D Play the following ostinato with your feet, and left hand playing cross stick (tip of the stick on the head near the rim and the shank of the stick on the rim itself) on the snare drum. Along with that, play the independence patterns with the right hand on a cowbell or the bell of the ride cymbal. This will help gain independence while playing a variety of Latin styles.

**Track 9 plays patterns 22–45.**

TRACK 9

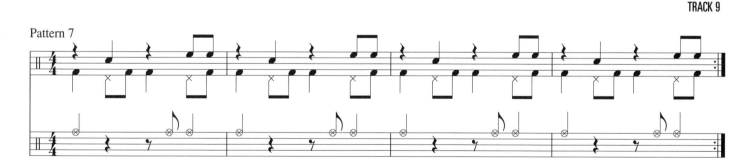

**E**  Now we will change the bass drum pattern in the ostinato and repeat what you did in application D, playing all of the independence patterns on the ride cymbal bell or a cowbell with the right hand. Applications D and E will prepare you for learning many Afro-Cuban, Caribbean, African, and Brazilian rhythms, as most of them contain one or more rhythmic ostinatos.

## Rock and Funk

Next we will look at some rock and funk applications for building independence in these styles.

**F**  In this application play a straight quarter-note rock feel with the right hand playing the hi-hat, left hand playing the snare drum, and the independence patterns on the bass drum.

**Track 10 plays patterns 1–21.**

Pattern 55

**Note:** Practice all of these applications at different tempos. You need to be able to make them groove at slow tempos, medium tempos, and fast tempos.

**G**  In the following, the hi-hat pattern is different from the previous pattern. It may be played with the right hand or left hand if you wish to develop ambidexterity. One may experiment with playing certain grooves "open handed"—left hand on the hi-hat and right hand on the snare drum. Play all of the independence patterns on the bass drum along with this ostinato.

Pattern 55

**H**  Two more hi-hat/snare drum ostinatos to be played with the independence patterns:

Pattern 84

Pattern 107

Keep in mind that it's important to practice all of these straight eighth-note grooves with a swing/triplet feel as well. A lot of funk, hip-hop, and rap music use these rhythms with a triplet feel!

Decades ago, many rock drummers couldn't swing because the majority of what they played was in a straight eighth-note feel. Jazz drummers couldn't play rock and certain styles of funk because they were so used to playing in a triplet feel (swinging) for the most part. The generation of drummers from the 1960s, onward, became much more versatile, and many have accomplished the ability to master both feels. Today, this is a must if you want to have a successful career as a drummer!

**I** Below is yet another hi-hat/snare drum ostinato to practice with the independence patterns. This one works particularly well for slow and medium tempos. At these tempos, the hi-hat is played with the right hand only, unless using the open-handed technique (left hand on HH, right hand on SD).

Pattern 116

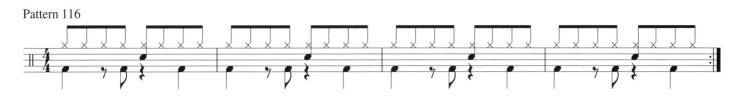

**J** This application is intended for medium fast and fast tempos. The hi-hat is played with right and left hands alternating. The snare drum is played with the right hand (see stickings below). Practice the independence patterns on the bass drum with this ostinato.

**Track 11 plays patterns 1–21.**

TRACK 11

Pattern 116

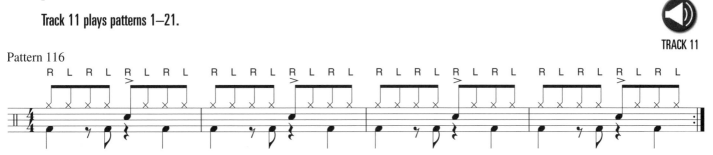

Remember, the end result you are going for with these exercises is to get them to the point where they either really swing or groove hard. I suggest that you practice the straight eighth-note feels with a click track at different tempos. This will improve your time exponentially.

## Advanced Patterns

Next, we will use some ostinatos that incorporate the ride cymbal while playing the hi-hat with your foot.

**K** Play the independence patterns on the bass drum while playing the ostinato shown below. This employs the use of the bell of the ride cymbal, the hi-hat played with foot, and the snare drum playing the backbeat.

Pattern 26

**L** Play the same ostinato as in letter K, but change the ride cymbal pattern. Play the bell of the cymbal on beats 2 and 4, while playing the independence patterns on the bass drum.

**M**  Play the ostinato below with the bass drum playing the independence patterns. Play the quarter notes on the bell of the ride cymbal and the eighth notes on the ride part of the cymbal.

**N**  Play the independence patterns on the bass drum with the following ostinato (accented notes are to be played on the bell of the ride cymbal).

**Track 12 plays patterns 118–141.**

TRACK 12

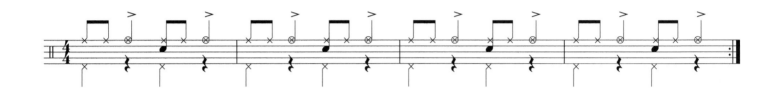

**O**  In the following, the left hand plays the independence patterns over two different funk ostinatos on an alternate snare drum, timbales, or bell set-up on the left side of your hi-hat.

Pattern 100

*Right hand plays the hi-hat and snare drum*

*Left hand plays the cowbell*

Pattern 71

*Right hand plays the ride cymbal and snare drum*

*Left hand plays the cowbell*

# 3 SOLO AND FILL APPLICATIONS

In this chapter we will explore some ways to use the independence patterns for solo applications, as well as getting around the drumset with the hands, while playing different ostinatos with the feet.

## Triplet Patterns

**A**  This application is in a triplet format. Play beats 2 and 4 on the hi-hat with your foot. Play alternating triplets (R, L, R, L, etc.) on the snare drum, starting with the right hand. Play the independence patterns as accents on the snare drum.

Pattern 8

**B**  Now play alternating triplets on the snare drum as before, starting with the right hand. Play the independence patterns on the floor tom (right hand) and the tom tom (left hand), and play the hi-hat on beats 2 and 4.

**Note:** By alternating the hands continuously, the tom you strike (high or floor) will depend on which hand is playing. Practice each pattern slowly to figure this out.

**Track 13 plays patterns 1–21.**

**TRACK 13**

Pattern 119

**C** Next, while playing alternating triplets on the snare drum, and beats 2 and 4 on the hi-hat, play the quarter notes of the independence patterns on the bass drum and ride cymbal. Play the eighth notes on the high tom and floor tom.

Pattern 122

These exercises are excellent for learning to get around the complete drumset in a triplet setting, using alternate sticking. Now let's use the independence patterns to work on getting around the drumset in an eighth-note feel. One thing to develop with these particular exercises is to be able to play them at medium tempos and build up your speed, so that you can cover a variety of different tempos.

## Straight Eighth-Note Patterns

**D** Play straight eighth notes on the snare drum (alternating, starting with the right hand). Play the hi-hat on beats 2 and 4 with the independence patterns on the snare drum as accents. Repeat the exercise starting with the left hand, also with alternate sticking.

Pattern 8

**E** Now play alternating eighth notes on the snare drum, starting with the right hand, and the independence patterns on the high tom (left hand) and floor tom (right hand). Keep the same hi-hat ostinato on beats 2 and 4. Repeat this exercise leading with the left hand.

Pattern 81

**F** Next, play beats 2 and 4 on the hi-hat, and alternating sticking on the snare drum, starting with the right hand. Play the independence patterns in the following manner: eighth notes on the high tom and floor tom, quarter notes on the bass drum and ride cymbal. Repeat the exercise, leading with the left hand (alternating sticking).

Pattern 94

## Clave Patterns

**G** The next few applications will help you to solo while playing left foot clave—on a jam block connected to a foot pedal via a stand made for this purpose. These stands are available from a number of percussion manufacturers. You may set your clave pedal on the left side of the hi-hat pedal. We will start by working with the 2/3 rhumba clave (notated below). Practice this pattern with the left foot until your time is steady.

2/3 Rhumba Clave

The clave pattern will be your ostinato for the next three applications. In this application, play alternating eighth notes on the snare drum starting with the right hand (alternating sticking) and play the independence patterns as accents on the snare drum, along with clave played with your left foot. (If you are interested to know more about clave and Latin rhythms, Horacio "el Negro" Hernandez has an excellent book out on this subject).

**Track 14 plays patterns 1–21.**

TRACK 14

Pattern 14

**H** While using clave as your ostinato, play eighth notes on the snare drum (alternating sticking), starting with the right hand, and play the independence patterns on the high tom (left hand) and floor tom (right hand).

Pattern 14

**I** In this application, while playing clave with the left foot, play the independence patterns as in application H, but play the quarter notes on the bass drum and cymbals, and the eighth notes on the high tom (left hand) and floor tom (right hand).

Pattern 14

You should also practice all of these clave/solo exercises with the 3/2 rhumba clave illustrated below.

3/2 Rhumba Clave

19

## Brushes

J   This application deals with brushes. Many good books are available on how to play the brushes. There is an exceptionally good video by Clayton Cameron entitled "The Living Art of Brushes." This video, and many of the books out there concerning brush technique, deal with different ways to play jazz time. What is lacking is a system to learn how to play accents and phrases in jazz with the brushes. Once you have learned how to play swing time on the snare drum with brushes, you can then use the independence patterns to practice playing accents. As a general rule, it may be easiest to play most of the accents that are on the downbeat, with the right hand. Consequently, most of the eighth notes on the "and" of the beat are easiest to play as an accent with the left hand, while keeping time on the snare drum. It is also good practice to play "two" and "four" on the hi-hat with your foot as part of this ostinato.

In your practice, the objective is to be able to play accents with the brushes on the snare drum while keeping fluid, solid time, and playing two and four on the hi-hat. You can go back to the beginning of this book and use almost all of the independence applications for jazz and apply them to the brushes, as well as the rest of the kit. For example, application letters B and D are a good place to start with brush independence after you have mastered playing time and phrasing with the brushes on the snare.

**Track 15 plays patterns 22–45.**

TRACK 15

Pattern 22

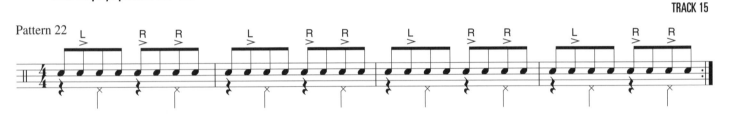

K   This next application involves an ostinato played on the snare drum and closed hi-hat with the hands, while playing the independence patterns on the bass drum. The sticking for the triplets is: R L L R L L R L L R L L. The snare drum is played with the right hand. Return to using drum sticks.

Pattern 117

L   Next we will look more in depth at developing the left hand to be independent from the other three limbs. Play the ostinato below with the independence patterns in your left hand on a cowbell (set up on the left side of the hi-hat) or on an alternate snare drum, or jam block (also set up on the left side of your hi-hat). Play the hi-hat and snare drum with your right hand only.

Pattern 118

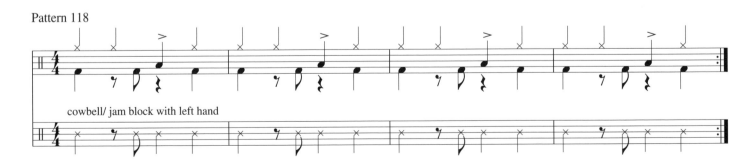

cowbell/ jam block with left hand

# 4 HAND/FOOT COORDINATION

## Short-Phrase Patterns

The following patterns are basic building blocks for solo and fill ideas. One of the best things about these exercises is that they involve the bass drum in all of the patterns. They are meant to be practiced at first, like rudiments: start slow and gradually build up speed until you reach your maximum. Then, gradually slow down to the speed at which you started. After you are comfortable with this application, be ready to use each pattern as a fill played in time: triplet feel and straight eighth-note feel. Below are the Hand-Foot Coordination patterns.

**Note:** When a pattern involves both hands, play the right hand on the floor tom and the left hand on the snare drum in order to get two sounds instead of one sound from the hands.

## Fills in Time

After you have mastered playing each of these patterns slow to fast to slow, begin to put them in time, as fills. In the following exercises, play two measures of time (swing ostinato) and two measures of the pattern as a fill. Let's begin with pattern number 1. (Keep the hi-hat going with your foot while playing the fill.)

Pattern 1 – Swing

Note: The rhythm has been changed to triplets, but the fill maintains the same alternating floor tom/bass drum pattern. The same is true with pattern number 2 below.

Pattern 2 – Swing

Practice all of the patterns in this way, playing time for two measures, and the pattern as a fill for two measures. Since you are using the swing ostinato, all of the patterns will be played as triplets regardless of how many notes there are in the pattern. For example, below is pattern number 16, which is a four-note pattern, used in a triplet format.

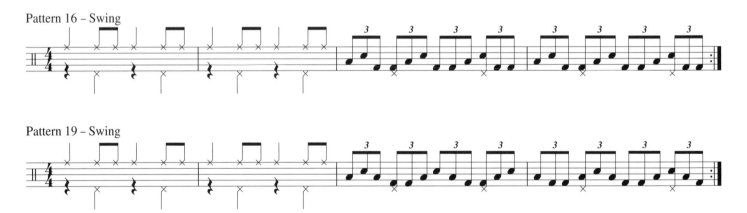

Pattern 16 – Swing

Pattern 19 – Swing

The next step is to practice these patterns at a faster tempo, playing them with a straight eighth-note feel. You can use the swing ostinato or a samba ostinato (same rhythm, but with straight eighth notes). As above, play two measures of time and two measures of the pattern as a fill, keeping the hi-hat going on beats 2 and 4. Play at a tempo of 208 beats per minute or faster.

Pattern 8 – Straight (no swing, fast tempo)

The following is an example using pattern number 20. Remember to play the floor tom with the right hand and the snare drum with the left hand.

Pattern 20 – Straight feel, fast tempo

Below is an example of one of many samba rhythms from Brazil. You can use this as your ostinato at a medium fast tempo for two measures, then play each hand-foot pattern for two measures. (Play cross stick on snare drum—tip of the stick on the head near the rim, and the shank of the stick on the rim itself.)

Pattern 18 Samba

The most difficult thing you may encounter in practicing these exercises is keeping the hi-hat going on beats 2 and 4, while playing each fill. You should also practice the patterns playing the hi-hat on beats 1, 2, 3, and 4, and then on beats 1 and 3 only. Then the next step is combining different patterns to hear how they sound as fills. You can start by combining pattern number 1 with all the other patterns. After that, combine pattern number 2 with all of the other patterns, then pattern 3, 4, etc.

## Short-Phrase Patterns in Consecutive Play

Another great exercise to practice with the hand/foot patterns is to play each one for four measures and, without stopping, move on to the next one until you have played them all. Then play the patterns in reverse order: start with the last pattern first (reading it backwards), play it four times, and keep going until you've reached pattern 1 as the last pattern. (Play the hi-hat on beats 1 and 3, then 2 and 4, and finally on all four beats—right hand on the floor tom, left hand on the snare drum, except on patterns that involve the hi-hat, i.e., 4, 5, and 6.)

In the following, the patterns are notated all in eighth notes, with each one lasting four measures. The brackets show the original pattern which is played until the four measures are up. Thus, certain patterns will begin and end at different places in the measure, such as pattern 19, which is only five notes long.

TRACK 16

On the blank staves below, try creating some of your own hand-foot coordination patterns.

## Displaced Patterns

All of the previous patterns can be displaced by an eighth note in time. A few examples of displaced patterns are shown below.

Pattern 1

In 1a, pattern 1 is displaced by one eighth note. The second note in the first measure becomes the first note of the displaced pattern.

Pattern 1a

If a pattern is three eighth notes in length, you can displace it 2 ways.

Pattern 11a

Pattern 11 displaced. The second note of the three-note pattern becomes the first note played.

Pattern 11b

In the following example, we see that the third note of pattern 11 is now the first note of the three-note phrase.

Pattern 11b

Next, we will displace pattern 18. Since it's a four-beat pattern, you can displace it three ways (not counting the way it is already written out, which makes four ways of playing it).

Pattern 18

Pattern 18a

Pattern 18b

Pattern 18c

The more notes there are in a pattern, the more times you can displace where you start that pattern.

26

# 5 ADVANCED STUDIES: SOLO AND FILL CONCEPTS

This section of the book deals with more adventurous fill and solo concepts. Many of the great contemporary drummers such as Dennis Chambers, Vinnie Colaiuta, Dave Weckl, and Steve Gadd, to name a few, have developed a way of playing solos and fills that astound drummers because of the speed and accuracy in which they play them. This chapter will attempt to take some of the mystery out of this unique concept as the language of the drumset continues to grow and develop.

## Triplet Fills in Swing

We will use the triplet pattern below as the first example for utilizing this concept. Practice it slowly at first, and work on speeding up the tempo until you can play it at 176 beats per minute (BPM).

Pattern A

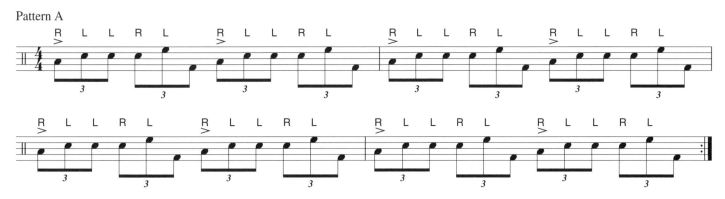

Many drummers learn a variety of patterns for fills, but usually begin and end them on the downbeat (first beat of the measure). The following examples illustrate the concept of starting a fill at different places in time, within the measure. The first four examples begin the fill at different places *on* the beat and examples 5–8 show the fills starting at different points in between the beat.

TRACK 17

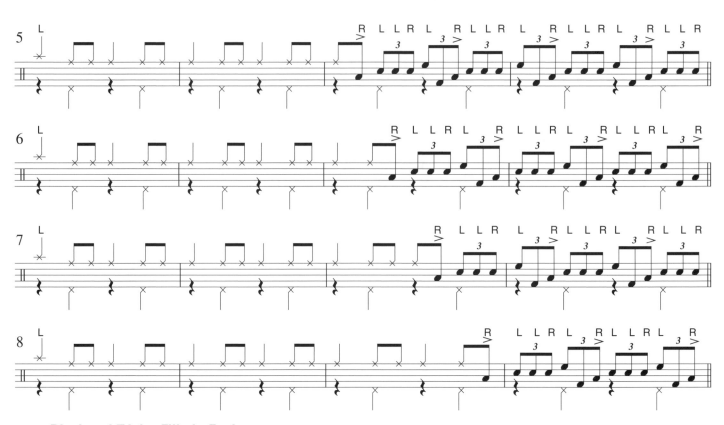

## Displaced Triplet Fills in Funk

Now, let's try using this concept in a funk context, starting the pattern on beat one, at a tempo of 100 BPM (hi-hat played with the hands).

Once you've mastered this, take a look at the following examples which show you how to displace this pattern so you can start it at different points in time, using the funk ostinato. We will also start to deal with accented notes in the pattern. When you accent certain notes in a displaced pattern, it helps the groove to stay focused on the quarter note. This cannot be stressed enough! What is the point of playing a fancy fill if the groove and time fall apart? If that is the case, it would be better not to play the fill at all. Particularly in pop, R&B, funk, Latin, and other groove oriented types of music, fills are essential to take the song from one section to another (for example, from the verse of a song to the bridge). Nevertheless, the fill has to flow, with good time and feel in order to accomplish this. In particular, all of the great studio drummers are aware of this fact.

TRACK 18

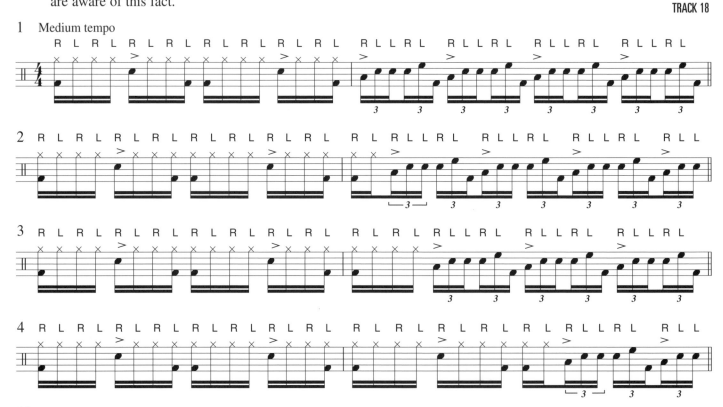

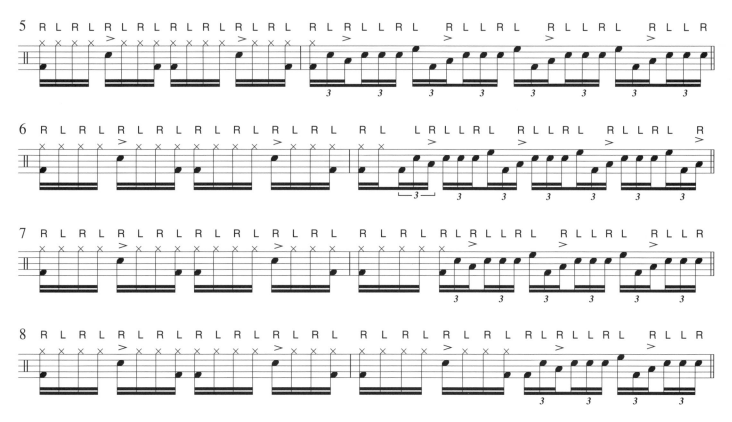

Continue to experiment, starting the pattern in different places within the measure.

## Mixed Fills in Swing, Funk, and Latin

Now, let's look at a different pattern.

Pattern B

Practice pattern B until you can play it at 176 BPM, then play it using all the different examples that you used with the first pattern using the swing ostinato and the funk ostinato. Once you have accomplished this, put patterns A and B together and displace them (start them in different places in time) in the same way that you did with each pattern by itself.

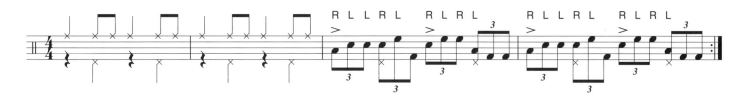

Next, play time, and start the pattern on beat 2 of the third measure. After that, start the pattern on beat 3 of the third measure. Lastly, start the pattern on beat 4 of the third measure. Below is an example showing the pattern starting on beat 4 of the third measure.

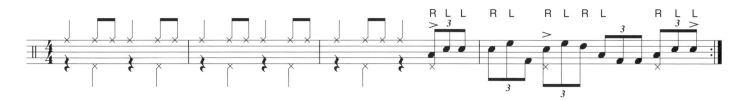

The next step is to take pattern A and apply it in an eighth-note concept. You can use a swing ostinato, funk ostinato, or samba ostinato to practice this concept. We will start out with a swing ostinato, showing how to displace this pattern by starting it on different places in the measures. Practice this exercise at 220 BPM or faster.

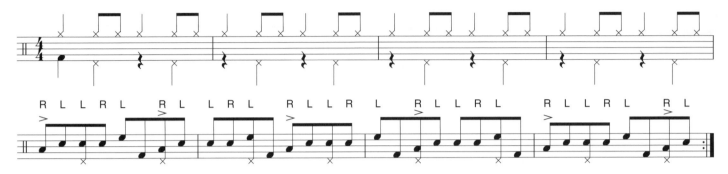

Next, start the pattern on the second eighth note of measure five.

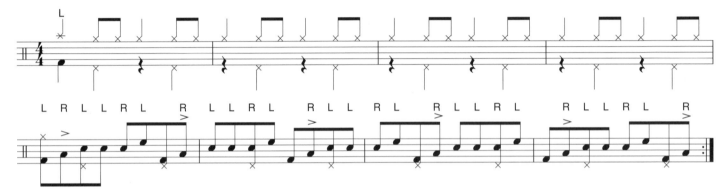

You should also start the pattern on the third eighth note of the fifth measure, then start it on the fourth eighth note, then the fifth eighth note. Continue in this fashion until you have displaced the pattern to where you are starting it on the first beat of measure eight.

In this next example, you will use a samba ostinato and start the pattern with a triplet/swing feel on the fourth beat of the third measure (244 BPM). Play the snare drum with a cross-stick.

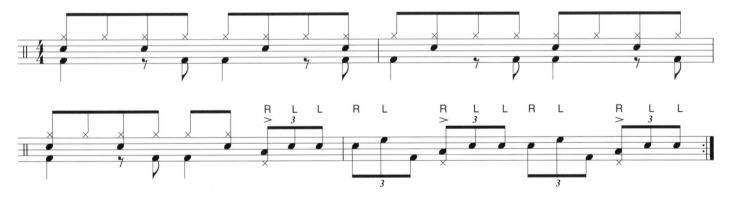

The next example starts the pattern with a straight eighth-note feel on the fourth eighth note of the third measure.

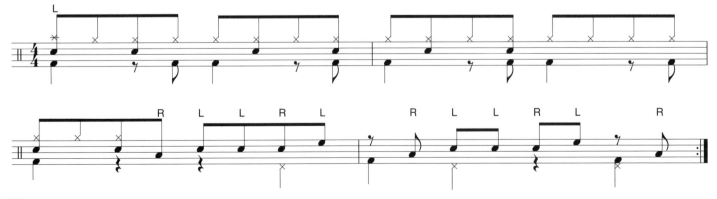

Below are a few additional triplet patterns that you can displace using the same concepts as in the previous examples. You are also encouraged to come up with your own patterns.

## Ending the Fill

So far, we have been dealing with starting patterns at different places in time (or measures) of music. Now let's address the possibilities of different places to end the patterns (or phrases).

A Up until now, we have been ending all of the patterns in the Advanced Studies chapter on the downbeat of one. The following examples will demonstrate how to end the pattern before the downbeat of the following measure (also known as an anticipation, in rhythmic terms) and also places in time "over the bar line," (after beat one of the next measure).

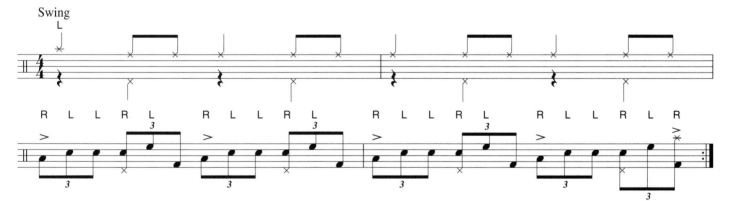

B The following shows the pattern ending over the bar line, on the last note of the first triplet in the first measure.

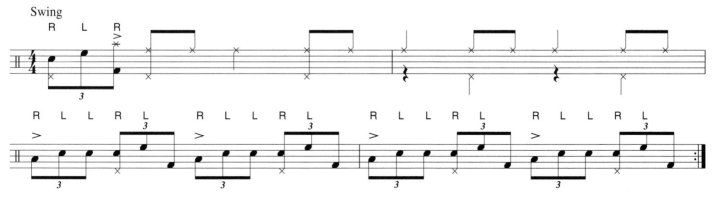

# 6 WARM-UP EXERCISES

There have been many instructional books, videos, and DVDs dealing with warm-up exercises. I just thought I'd share some of mine with you. It's a routine I try to do every day. Consistency with practice is the key to success. Enjoy!

The following exercises apply to traditional and match grip styles of playing. The first warm-up one can do is finger control exercises. They help build the muscles in the forearm that control each finger in the hand. The most important part of this grip is the "fulcrum"—the place where you hold the stick between your thumb and index finger (match grip).

The following pages present a system for developing the fingers and muscles that control them.

**f** = fulcrum, **m** = middle finger, **r** = ring finger, **l** = little finger.

Below is a system of 16th note exercises played in the following ways: with the fulcrum only, with each finger individually, and with all fingers at the same time (how the exercise should end up). When using the middle, ring, and little fingers to move the stick, make sure you always hold the stick with the fulcrum as well. Try to use only your fulcrum and fingers, but as little wrist as possible. Play each pattern four times, then move on to the next one. (If you play match-grip, play through these patterns first with your left hand, then your right hand. If you play traditional grip exclusively, practice this exercise with your right hand only). Try to start this exercise at 60 BPM using a metronome or some other device, and, over a period of time, work your speed up to 80 BPM.

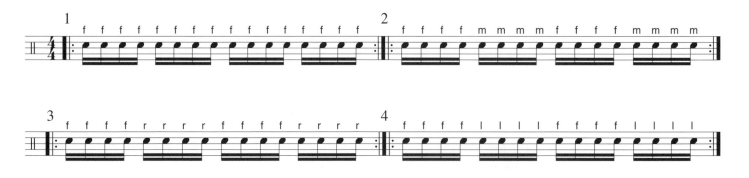

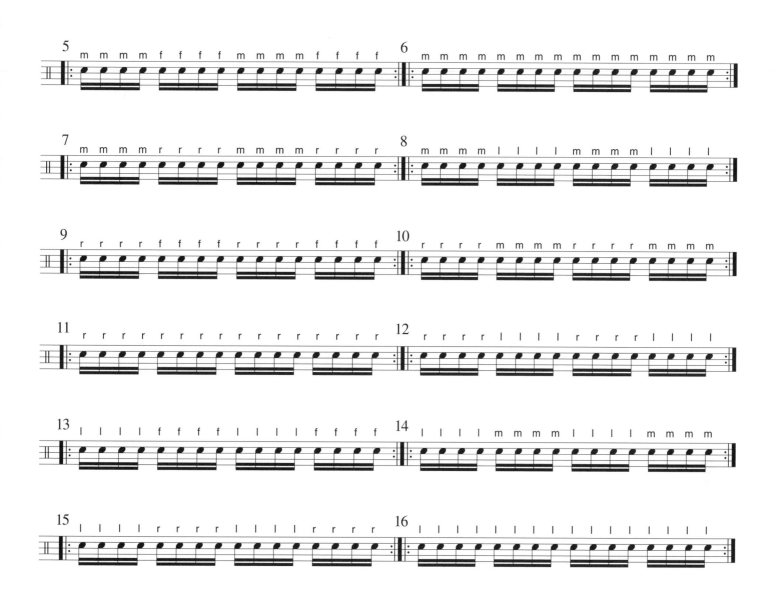

For traditional-grip warm-ups, turn your left hand clockwise until the stick is under your hand with the tip over the center of the pad. It's the same kind of motion with the left hand that you would make if you had a small amount of sugar in your palm and wanted to transfer it to a tabletop. In the beginning, your palm should be facing up; at the end, your palm will be facing down toward the table top. Play four sixteenth notes to the beat using only the index finger to move the stick to the pad. Do this for four measures, then switch to the middle finger, also playing four measures of 16th notes. Your fulcrum is the part of your hand right below your index finger and the thumb. Never let this part of the grip go. That doesn't mean that you have to hold it really tight—the looser the better. Do your best to move the stick with your index finger, then your middle finger in this over-hand position. This will strengthen the muscles in your forearm that control these two fingers. Strength here is necessary, in that these two fingers are instrumental in making the traditional grip technique work economically and correctly.

## Sticking Exercises

The next exercises to do in the warm-ups are a series of stickings, played on a practice pad with a metronome. Please find the complete sticking exercises on the following pages. I will list BPM times at certain intervals. Play four 16th notes to each metronome click.

**96 BPM**

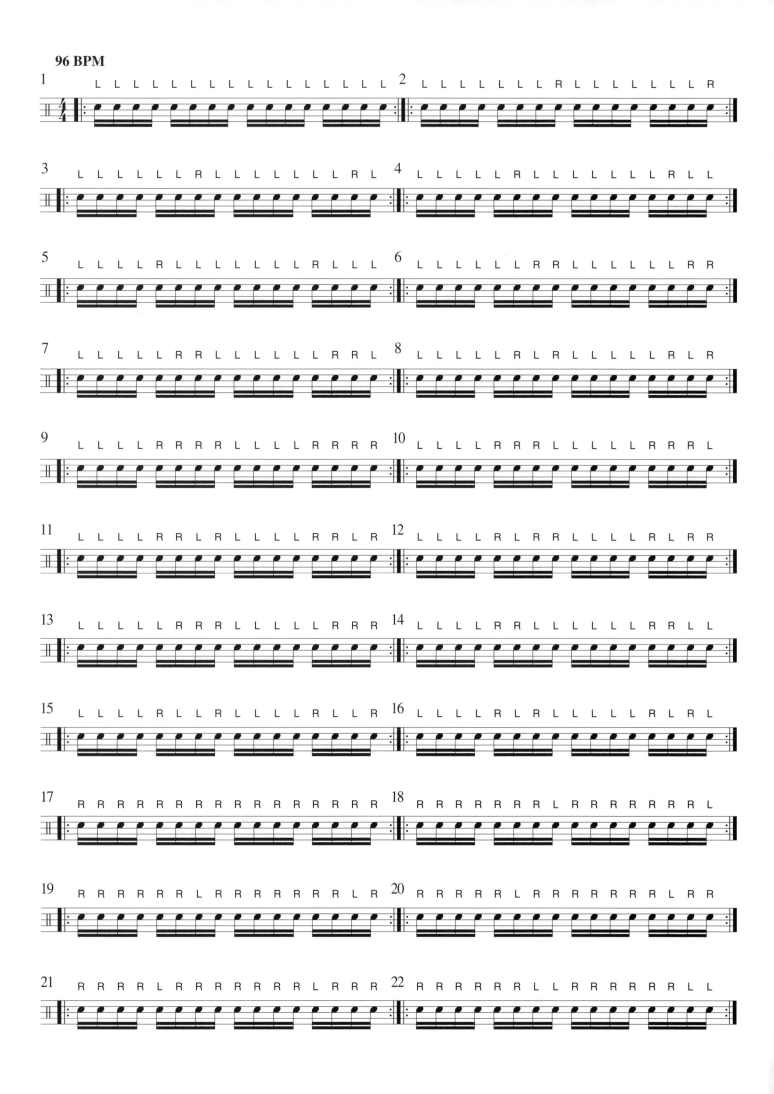

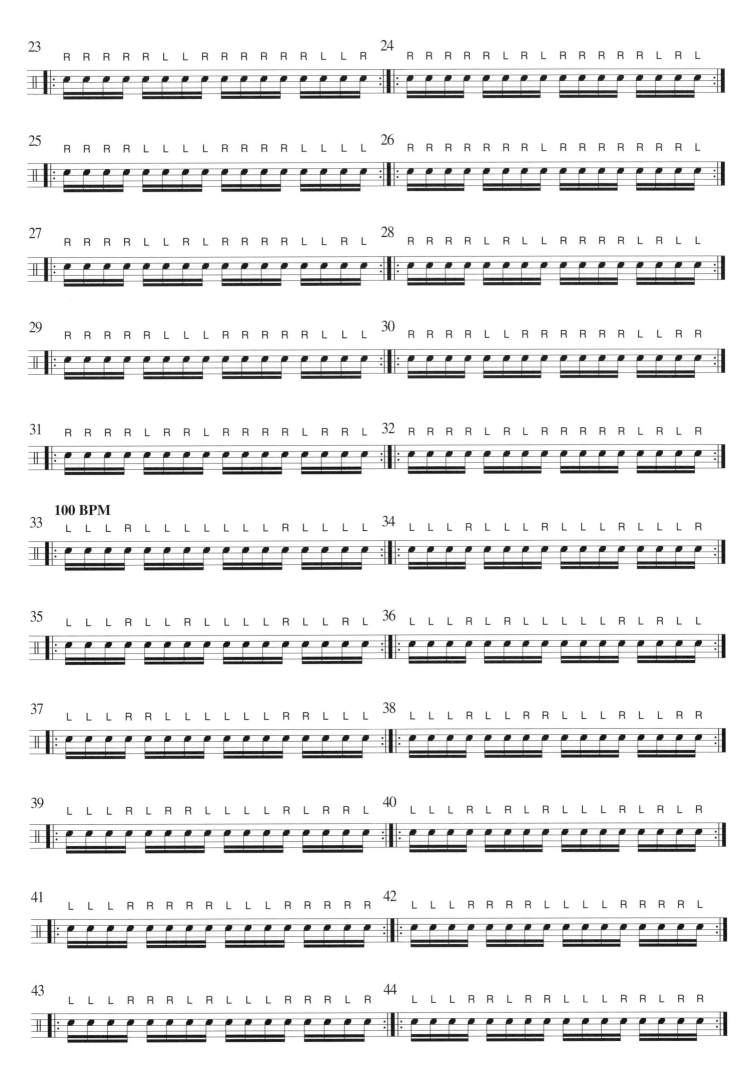

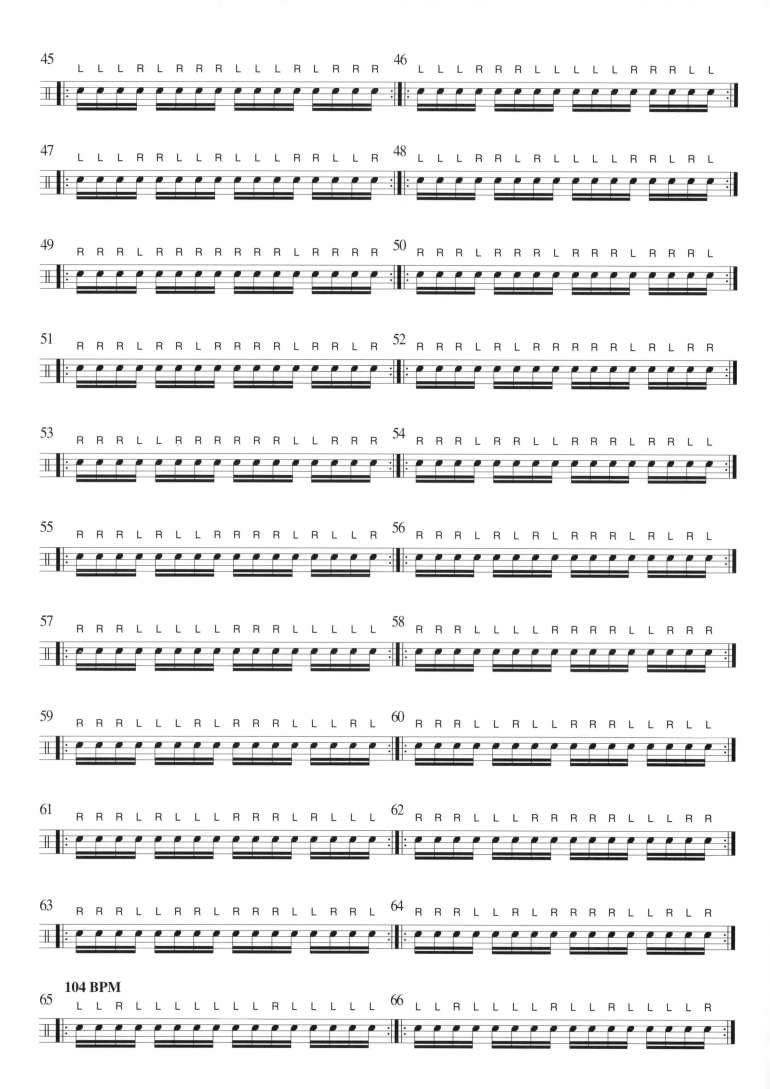

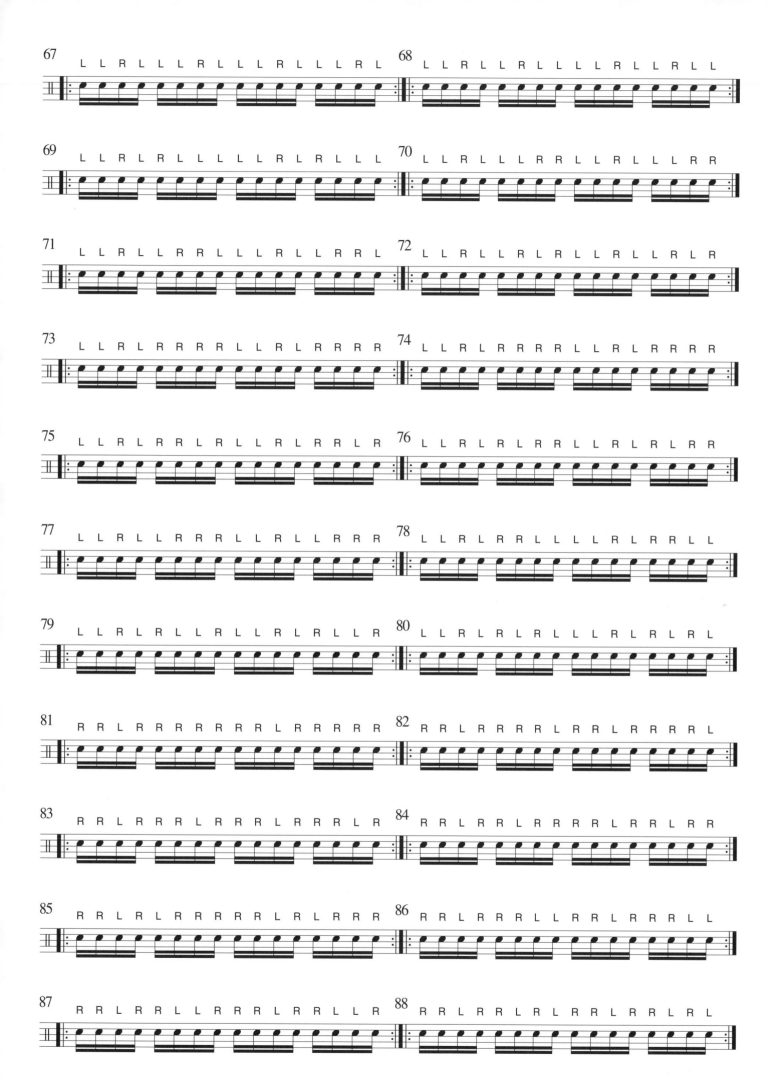

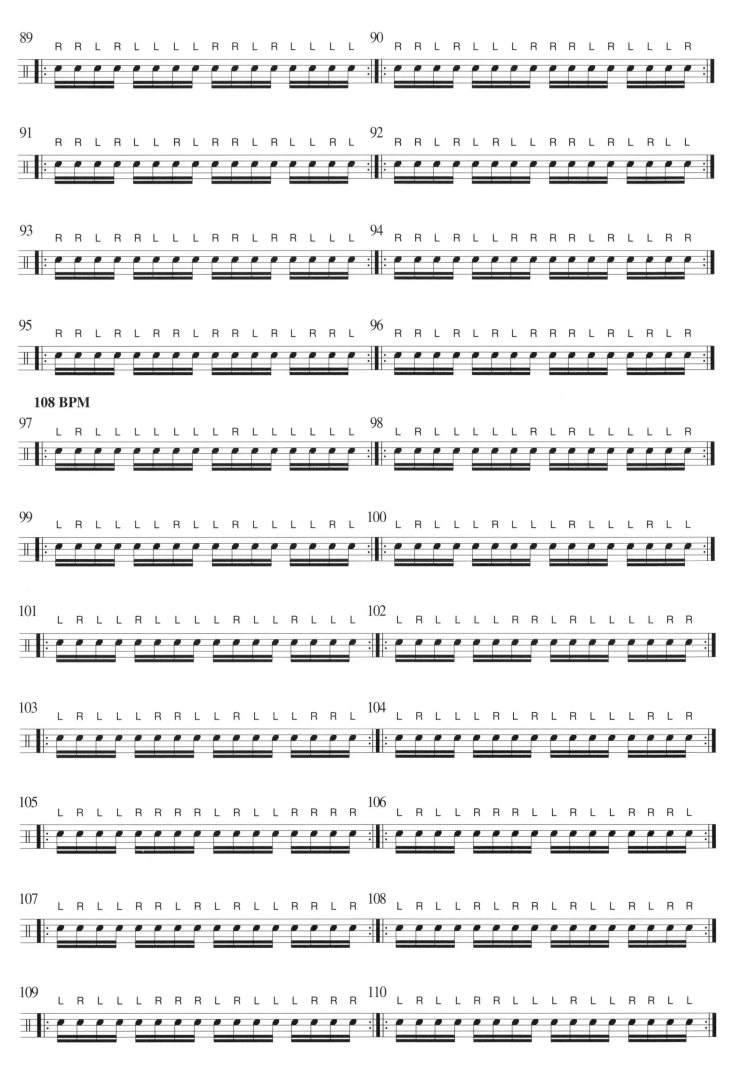

**108 BPM**

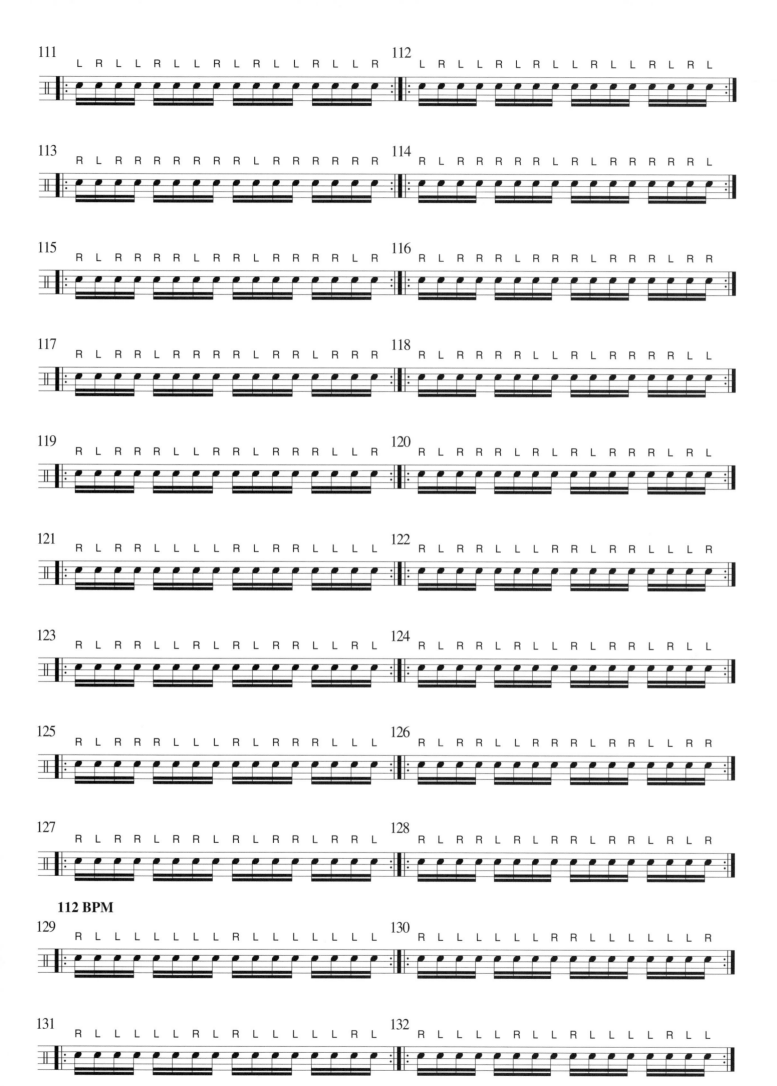

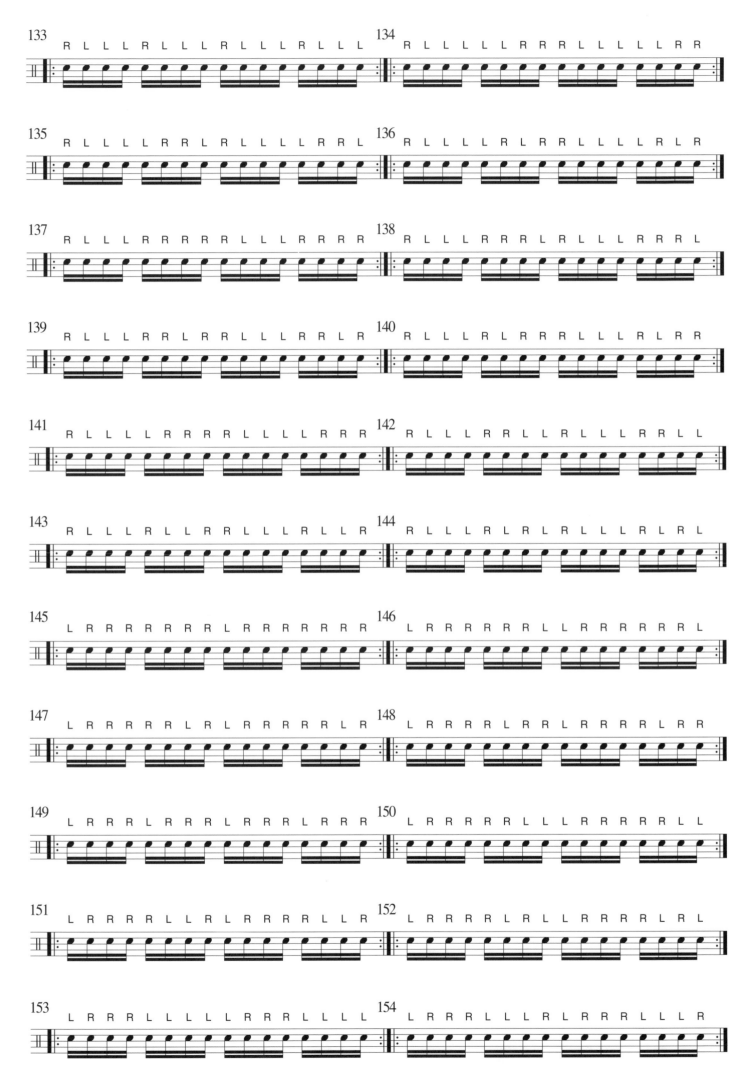

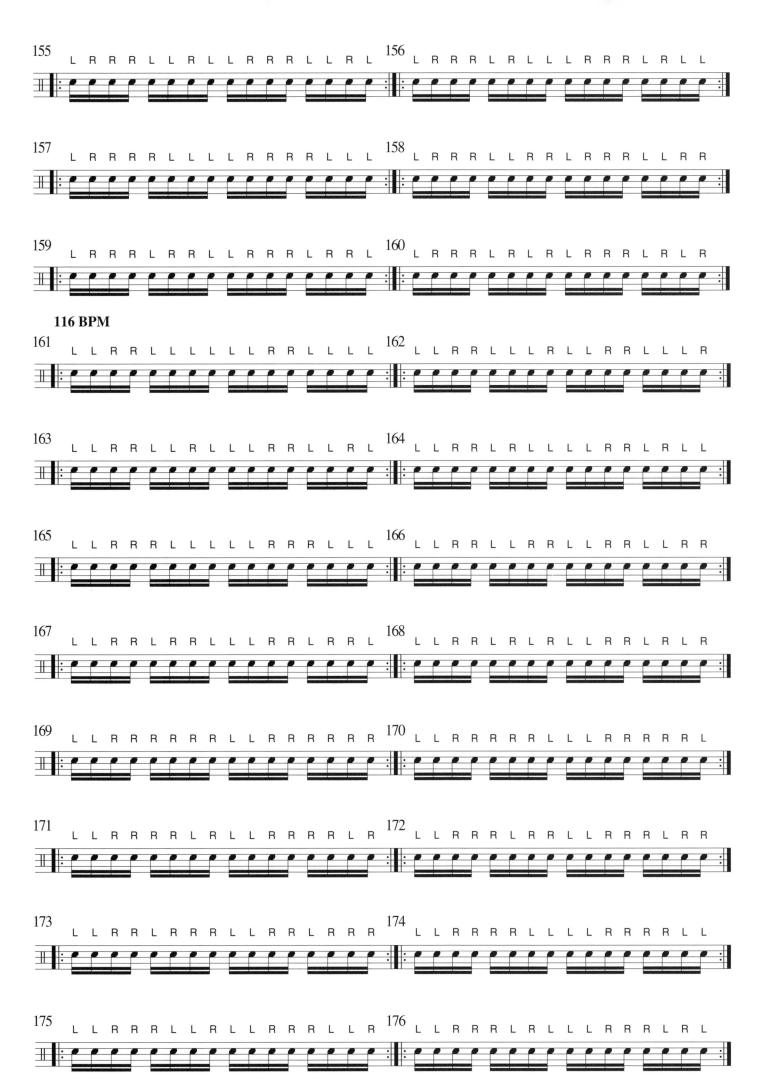

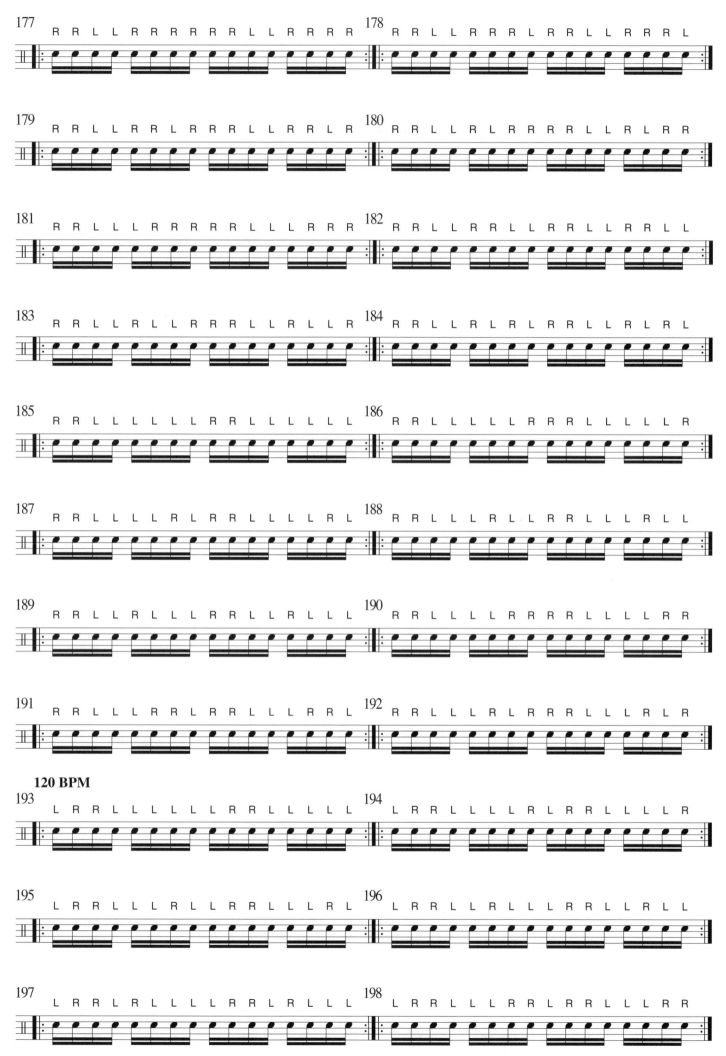

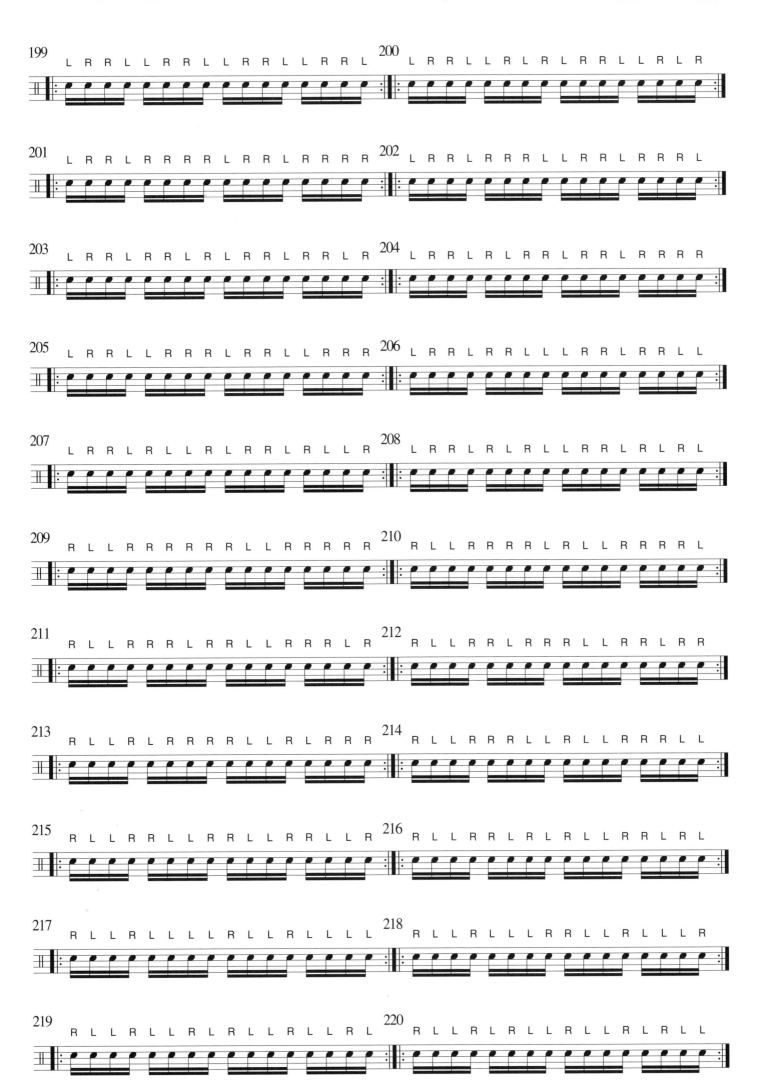

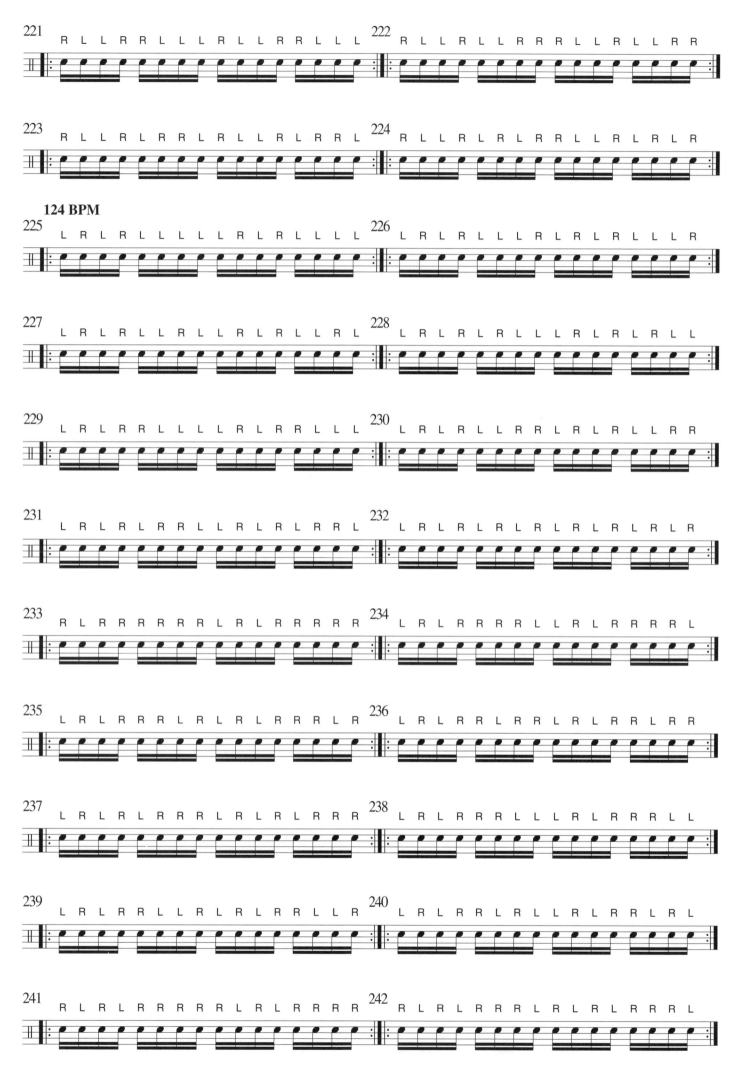

243
R L R L R R L R R L R L R L R R L R

244
R L R L R L R L R R R L R L R L R L R R

245
R L R L L R R R R L R L R L L R R R

246
R L R L R R L L R L R L R L R R L L

247
R L R L R L L R R L R L R L R L L R

248
R L R L R L R L R L R L R L R L R L

249
R L R L L L L L R L R L R L L L L L

250
R L R L L L L R R L R L R L L L L R

251
R L R L L L R L R L R L L L R L

252
R L R L L R L L R L R L L L R L L

253
R L R L R L L L R L R L R L R L L L

254
R L R L L L R R R L R L L L L R R

255
R L R L L L R R L R L R L L R R L

256
R L R L L R L R R L R L L L R L R

45

# 7 WORLD MUSIC RHYTHMS

In this chapter you will find rhythms from south Louisiana (particularly from New Orleans and southwest Louisiana [Cajun & Zydeco]), Brazil, Cuba, Puerto Rico, and other areas of the Caribbean. These are beats that I have learned and/or created for different recording artists. I feel that every professional drummer should know these rhythms and the musical cultures that they come from. It will only enhance what you already know on the drumset.

## NEW ORLEANS SECOND LINE GROOVES

Below you will find a series of snare drum patterns and bass drum/hi-hat patterns. First, master playing the snare drum patterns, then master the BD/HH patterns. Once you have accomplished this, take snare pattern 1 and practice it with all of the BD/HH patterns. Then do the same with snare pattern 2, then 3, etc. Play the eighth notes with a triplet/swing feel.

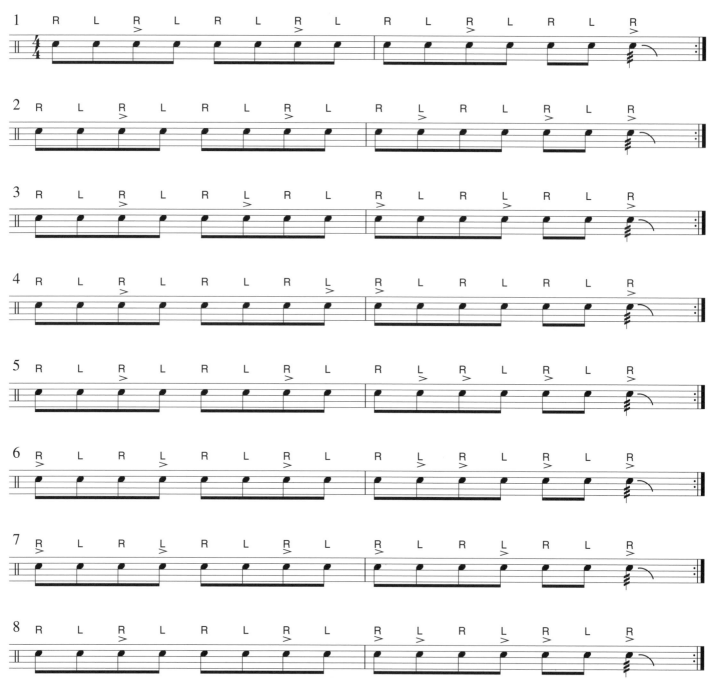

In the beginning of the 1900s, before the bass drum pedal was invented, African Americans took European instruments and put together brass bands that performed for many different functions. The drum section in the brass bands in New Orleans consisted of a snare drummer and a bass drummer. The bass drummer attached a small cymbal onto the top of the bass drum shell and played it with a metal coat hanger or other device. Below are some traditional bass drum/splash cymbal patterns. Practice these closing the hi-hat completely and also splashing the hi-hat (done by striking the rear of the pedal with the heel of the foot).

**Track 19 plays bass drum/hi-hat patterns 1–10 with snare drum pattern 1.**

TRACK 19

# BRAZILIAN RHYTHMS

Brazil is such a large country, populated by so many different ethnic groups that many different styles of music and rhythms have developed there since the country's inception. I will start with samba, and also cover other rhythms such as partido-alto, baião, frevo, afoxe, batucada (a form of samba played by large percussion groups during Carnival in Rio de Janeiro), and Samba-Funk. A very important aspect of this music is that it is felt and written in 2/4 time, not 4/4 time.

## Samba

In the following exercises, play the closed hi-hat with the right hand and the snare drum with the left hand (cross-stick, tip of the stick on the drumhead). Practice these rhythms at different tempos; slow, medium, fast, and faster!

In the patterns below, the snare drum is played with a feel that is not straight sixteenth notes or a triplet feel, but in between the two feels. That's what gives this music the unique swing that it has. Listen to the CD example of this groove and some Brazilian music. Practice along to help get the feel.

Track 20 plays patterns 1–4, consecutively.

TRACK 20

## Samba Funk

I highly recommend getting some Brazilian CDs by artists such as Airto Moriera, Flora Purim, Djavan, Ivan Lins, Elis Regina, to name a few, so that you can hear how the following grooves are used in Brazilian music. (The hi-hat is played with the right hand and the snare drum is played either open or with a cross-stick.) The first snare drum note is optional. You may play the first snare note at the beginning of the song and later as a variation.

**Track 21 plays all three patterns, consecutively.**

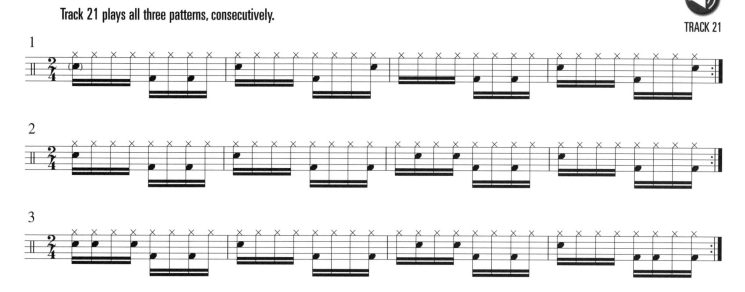

TRACK 21

## Batucada Samba

Batucada is where modern-day samba comes from. Batucada is the Brazilian equivalent of the American marching bands and drum corps, and New Orleans Second Line brass bands. A batucada group consists of many members playing traditional Brazilian percussion instruments. They march during Carnival in Rio de Janeiro with a panel of judges in attendance to present first place to whichever group is selected as the winner. Below are some adaptations of these rhythms on the drumset. (Listen to the CD to hear how the sixteenth notes on the snare drum are to be felt when played).

**Track 22 plays patterns 1–3, consecutively.**

TRACK 22

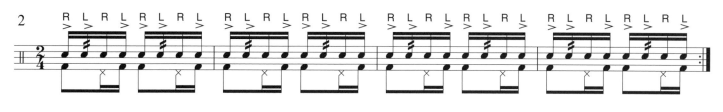

In the next two batucada patterns, play a buzz roll with the left hand on the second sixteenth note of each beat.

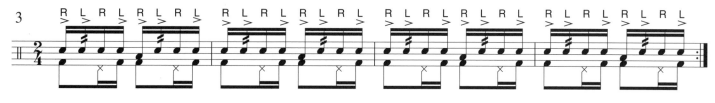

## Baião

Baião is a rhythm from Bahia in the northeast of Brazil. Traditionally, this music was played with percussion instruments, and was later adapted to the drumset. Practice this at 104 BPM and faster. Since the triangle is a major percussion instrument in baião, play on the bell of the hi-hat to simulate that sound. Use the tip of the sticks on the sixteenth notes and the shank of the stick on the eighth note (played open with the right hand).

**Track 23 plays patterns 1–3, consecutively.**

TRACK 23

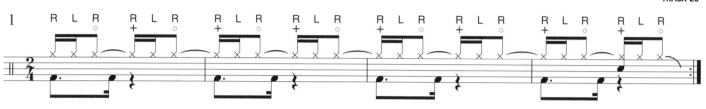

This example of baião is played on the ride cymbal. The snare drum is played as ghost notes, except where accented.

The following is ride cymbal, snare drum variation.

## Partido Alto

Partido alto is a rhythm similar to clave in Afro-Cuban music in that it is a two bar pattern (in 2/4 time) that can be switched so that the second measure of the pattern becomes the first measure, and the first measure of the original pattern becomes the second measure of the new two-bar pattern. It is a form of displacement using measures instead of specific beats. The first example is partido alto starting on the downbeat and, in the second example, the pattern starts on the "and" of one. (The second measure becomes the first measure in example 2).

**Track 24 plays patterns 1–4, consecutively.**

TRACK 24

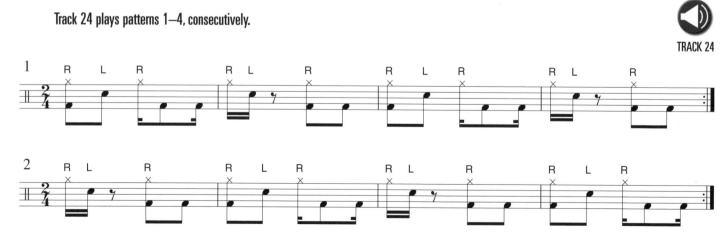

Number 3 below is an alternate hi-hat or ride cymbal pattern.

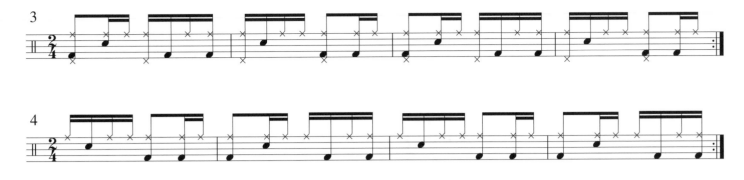

## Afoxe

Afoxe is a Brazilian "street parade" rhythm, similar to the samba. In the first example, the hi-hat is played with the right hand and the snare drum with the left hand. Open the hi-hat on the "and" of beats 1 and 2 of each measure. The snare drum can be played open or cross-stick (tip of the stick on the head and the butt end of the stick on the rim.) Practice these rhythms at 84–112 BPM.

TRACK 25

TRACK 26

TRACK 27

In the next example, flange the hi-hat with your foot, opening it on the downbeat and closing it on the "and" of the beat.

TRACK 28

*Play 4 times*

## Frevo

Frevo, a popular dance rhythm in Brazil, is generally played at a fast tempo (112–138 BPM). There is an amazing similarity between this rhythm and a rhythm from a popular New Orleans song about the big chief of a Mardi Gras (New Orleans Carnival) Indian tribe, composed by Professor Longhair entitled "Big Chief."

Next, we have a bass drum variation.

The following is the beat from the song "Big Chief" by Professor Longhair from New Orleans. Notice the similarity in the snare drum pattern.

# LATIN GROOVES

Below are a few examples of Latin grooves adapted to the drumset from Afro-Cuban, salsa, & Latin jazz styles. Traditionally (before the advent of the drumset) this music utilized only percussion instruments such as congas, bongos, cowbells, claves, guiro, timbales, and wood blocks, to name a few. Afro-Cuban music, in particular, is based on clave (which means "key" in Spanish). Depending on the song, the rhythm may be played in 2/3 clave or 3/2 clave. There are two kinds of clave, son clave and rhumba clave and the rhythms are played on a percussion instrument called claves. Below, I have written each type of clave in 2/3 and 3/2 form.

## Clave

2/3 Son Clave

3/2 Son Clave

2/3 Rhumba Clave

3/2 Rhumba Clave

## Songo

Songo was actually the first style/genre of music in Cuba where the rhythms were developed for the drum-set specifically. A man named Juan Formell, bassist and bandleader of the group "Los Van Van," was responsible for this development in 1969. There has been a great misconception that the drummer Changuito invented songo, but he replaced the original drummer in Los Van Van in 1970 and has said (to his credit) that he did not invent songo. This style of Latin drumming has become very popular worldwide in the last 20 years. Play the clave pattern on the hi-hat with your foot or on an extra foot pedal attached to a jam block. Thanks to my good friend & great drummer Bobby Sanabria for the correct historical information about the creation of songo.

TRACK 29

1   2/3 Rhumba Clave

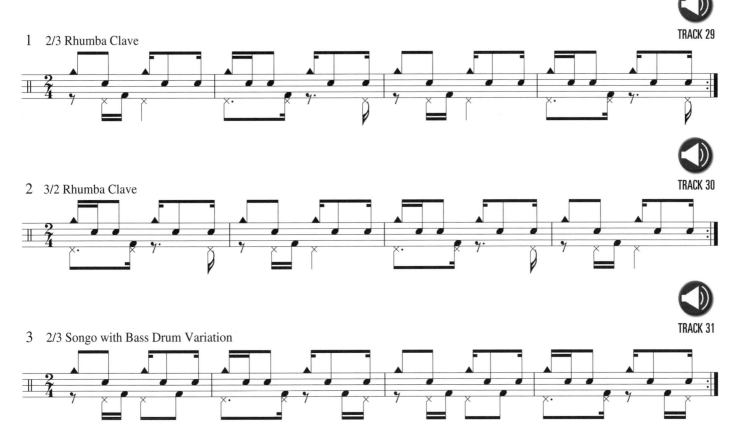

TRACK 30

2   3/2 Rhumba Clave

TRACK 31

3   2/3 Songo with Bass Drum Variation

In this next variation, the right hand plays on the side of the floor tom and the left hand plays cross-stick on the snare drum to simulate the rhythm that would normally be played by the timbalero on the sides of the timbales.

4

## Guaguanco

Traditionally played on percussion instruments, this is an adaptation of guaguanco to the drumset. First, let's look at the cascara rhythm that is essential to many Latin beats. It is played on the side of the floor tom with the right hand.

Cascara with 2/3 Rhumba Clave

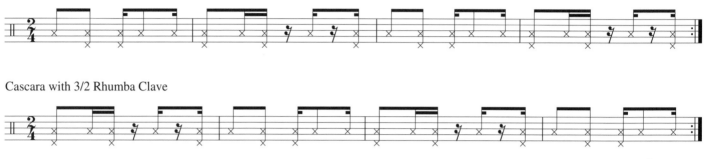

Cascara with 3/2 Rhumba Clave

When playing guaguanco without a percussionist, try to incorporate as many of the percussion parts as possible onto the drumset. Play the cascara pattern on the side of the floor tom with the right hand. Play the toms and snare drum (cross-stick) with the left hand. Play clave on a jam block with your left foot, but you can also play clave on the hi-hat with your left foot or just play on beats 1 and 2.

1 Guaguanco with 3/2 Clave

TRACK 32

2 Guaguanco with 2/3 Clave

3

The next example is a guaguanco with cross-stick on the snare drum.

Below is a Latin groove that I came up with and used on many recordings and performances. It has elements of different Latin rhythms and I call it an "all purpose" Latin groove. The right hand plays the cascara pattern on the side of the floor tom and the left hand plays the snare drum (cross-stick) and the hi-tom.

Here is another Latin groove that I developed for the drumset using a mambo bell pattern instead of the cascara pattern played on the side of the floor tom.

# Calypso

Calypso is a style of music from Trinidad and Tobago. Their culture also celebrates Carnival at the same time as Brazil, Cuba, Puerto Rico, and Louisiana. Calypso music is augmented by the beautiful sound of steel pans and steel drums. These instruments, made from a metal oil drum, are the most recent chromatic instruments invented in the history of musical instruments. A man named Ellie Manette is credited with their creation. Another unique percussion instrument used in this music is the brake drum (the metal wheel from a car). Calypso is an Afro-Centric music that is also played and felt in 2/4 time. One American jazz artist that made this beat very popular in the U.S. is Sonny Rollins, with his composition "St. Thomas." The hi-hat is played with the right hand and the snare drum, and toms are played with the left hand (unless you want to play left handed, which makes it easier to play the snare and tom parts).

# CAJUN AND ZYDECO

Cajun and Zydeco music originated in Southwest Louisiana in an area known as the Acadian Triangle. Cajuns, or Acadians (Cajun is slang for Acadian) are of French and American Indian descent. The French discovered the island off the eastern coast of Canada that is now known as Nova Scotia (New Scotland). They lived there in peace with the Micmac Indian tribes. Several Acadians and Micmacs married and raised families. The English arrived and claimed the land because the Acadians refused to sign a proclamation honoring the king of England as their king. As a result, the English split up the families, put them on different ships, and dropped them off as indentured servants in Maine, Maryland, the Carolina's, Georgia, and as slaves in the West Indies where they worked alongside the Africans. This went on for thirty years until they were released and relocated in Louisiana. Many Africans went with them. Cajun music is music of the Acadians and Zydeco is the music of the Africans that moved to Louisiana. It traditionally consisted of the following instruments: accordion, violin, triangle, and spoons, played on the knee with two hands. Zydeco music instrumentation originally consisted of accordion, washboard, triangle, and violin. When the drumset was invented, both cultures adopted it into their music. The washboard is still used extensively in both styles.

## Cajun Grooves

Play the bell of the hi-hat cymbal to simulate the triangle. The hi-hat is played with the right hand and the snare drum is played with the left hand. The following grooves have a straight eighth-note feel.

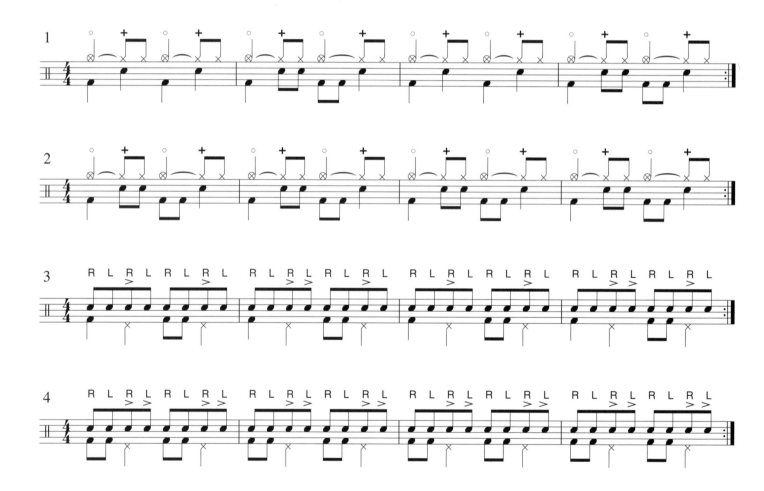

## Zydeco Grooves

Zydeco rhythms are similar to Cajun rhythms, especially patterns 3 and 4 on the previous page. The big difference is that many sidecar rhythms are played with a shuffle (triplet) feel as demonstrated below. (Interpret the eighth notes with a triplet feel as you did with the independence patterns using the swing ostinato.)

## Cajun/Zydeco Waltz

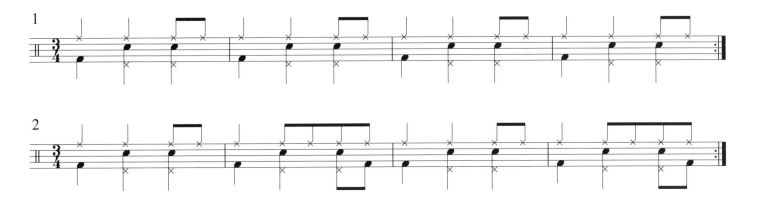

# INDEPENDENCE PATTERNS

You may wish to copy these pages and place them on your wall or a stand for easier access.

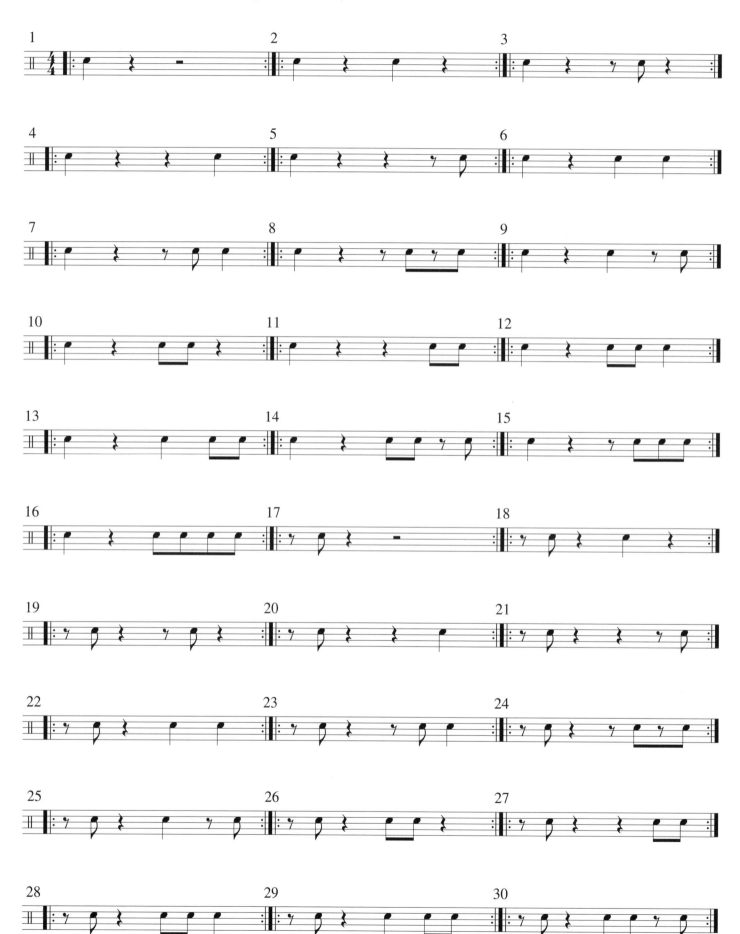